YO-CAZ-363

EQUITY 101

The EQUITY FRAMEWORK

BOOK 1

CURTIS LINTON

Foreword by BONNIE M. DAVIS

CORWIN

A SAGE Publishing Company

CORWIN
A SAGE Publishing Company

FOR INFORMATION:

Corwin

A SAGE Company

2455 Teller Road

Thousand Oaks, California 91320

(800) 233-9936

Fax: (800) 417-2466

www.corwin.com

SAGE Ltd.

1 Oliver's Yard

55 City Road

London EC1Y 1SP

United Kingdom

SAGE India Pvt. Ltd.

B 1/I 1 Mohan Cooperative Industrial Area

Mathura Road, New Delhi 110 044

India

SAGE Asia-Pacific Pte. Ltd.

33 Pekin Street #02-01

Far East Square

Singapore 048763

Acquisitions Editor: Dan Alpert

Associate Editor: Megan Bedell

Editorial Assistant: Sarah Bartlett

Production Editor: Amy Schroller

Copy Editor: Gretchen Treadwell

Typesetter: C&M Digitals (P) Ltd.

Proofreader: Victoria Reed-Castro

Indexer: Jean Casalegno

Cover Designer: Rose Storey

Permissions Editor: Karen Ehrmann

Copyright © 2011 by Curtis Linton

All rights reserved. When forms and sample documents are included, their use is authorized only by educators, local school sites, and/or noncommercial or nonprofit entities that have purchased the book. Except for that usage, no part of this book may be reproduced or utilized in any form or by any means, electronic or mechanical, including photocopying, recording, or by any information storage and retrieval system, without permission in writing from the publisher.

Printed in the United States of America

Library of Congress Cataloging-in-Publication Data

Linton, Curtis.

Equity 101—Book 1 : The Equity framework / Curtis Linton; foreword by Bonnie M. Davis.

p. cm.
Includes bibliographical references.

ISBN 978-1-4129-9517-7 (pbk.)

1. Educational equalization—United States—Case studies. I. Title. II. Title: Equity framework.

LC213.2.L56 2011
379.2'60973—dc22   2011001809

Certified Chain of Custody
Promoting Sustainable Forestry
www.sfiprogram.org
SFI-01268

SFI label applies to text stock

This book is printed on acid-free paper.

18 19 20 21 22 10 9 8 7 6 5 4 3

The EQUITY FRAMEWORK

*This book is dedicated to the two most
amazing kids I could ever hope to father, and
the loving mother who is raising them.*

*Dominic and Maya, I write this for you so that
the schools you attend can fulfill the limitless potential
you show every day. The two of you actualize my dreams.*

*Melody, I can only write this because of who you are as a person,
as a teacher, as a mother, and as my partner.
I am better because of you.*

Contents

Foreword

Curtis Linton is both an outsider and an insider. As an outsider, he observes educators through the lens of a camera and the pen of an author. He has no degree in education, yet he has been in more than two thousand classrooms and hundreds of schools to record what he finds. He has seen more than most educators.

As an insider, Curtis Linton is a White male who fits the norms of the middle-class, White person in our society. If you saw him in the halls of your school, you might assume he is a principal or a teacher. He appears a bit young to be a superintendent.

Yet, within his most intimate relationships, Curtis is again an outsider. He is a father of two children of Color, and he must watch them navigate experiences he will never have while he supports them from the outside. At the same time, Curtis possesses a unique view of race and racism since he views it through the prism of privilege while watching two beautiful children actualize the messages they receive from the media, their teachers, and their peers.

Curtis is both an outsider and an insider, and therein lies the uniqueness of his perspective in this book. Because Curtis views what occurs in classroom after classroom and school after school and district after district as an outsider, he brings a fresh perspective—a perspective of one who sees from both the outside and the inside. In this *Equity 101,* he offers that knowledge by presenting both a framework for the journey to understand equity and the tools with which to achieve it. According to Curtis, he is a White person who passionately believes we must "center ourselves in equity," and create educational institutions where students "can self-actualize their own future success."

In *Equity 101,* Curtis accomplishes many things; however, two things are especially meaningful for our understanding of how equity exists or does not exist in our schools. First, he looks at himself to understand better the role he plays in hindering or promoting equity in education. While documenting his own history, he digs deeply into the consciousness of the White male who is an insider in our society, yet who comes from a religious background, Mormonism, that has caused him to be perceived as an outsider. He shares his deepest fears, embarrassments, prejudices, and humiliations along with his greatest joys. In addition, he tells us how he and his wife transformed their daily experiences by bringing two children of Color into their lives. He shares his highest hopes and dreams for them—hopes and dreams not unlike those of any loving father who wants the best for his children. Once again, we learn about Curtis as both the outsider and the insider who has a reason for sharing his story. Curtis shares his personal story in order for us to engage in our own excavation of our deepest fears, embarrassments, prejudices, and humiliations centered upon race. This is a step in the process to understanding equity, and as White people in our society, if we never take this journey, we "deflect the conversation," as Curtis says, and remain inured to our own complicity in the racial story of our society.

The second thing Curtis does in *Equity 101* is offer a foundation for change: an Equity Framework, an online community, and strategies proven in the schools to have closed the gap. *Equity 101* is the foundation and the first book in a series of four books to address this issue, provide a map for the journey to equity, and establish our work within a community where we can share our collective challenges and successes. This series provides us with support for closing the educational inequity gaps and creates a climate for equity in our school districts.

Curtis is committed to sharing the hard stuff that creates barriers between White folks of privilege and people of Color. He is committed to sharing the strategies that begin to break down barriers. He is committed to working with White people to further emphasize that we White people need to do our race work on ourselves; we should not expect people of Color to "fix" us. We need to not opt out when the work becomes uncomfortable, difficult, and bereft of progress. Instead, we must find ways to support each other as we dig deeper inside our psychic wounds and expose our roadblocks:

whether they be prejudices, racist thoughts and actions, or instances of our own privilege.

Curtis says "the purpose of engaging in this process of centering one's self in equity is simple: if you do not understand deeply your own realities, it is very hard to help others—such as your students—successfully negotiate their own realities." So much of it is about understanding our own realities, and Curtis not only models how to do that in *Equity 101,* but gives us the tools to go beyond the modeling and engage in the process.

Curtis clearly defines the purpose of this book: "to define equity, illustrate it clearly, and illuminate its impact on student learning through the stories of highly successful schools and school systems that are eliminating their achievement gaps and lifting all students to high levels of success." Unlike other books focused solely on equity, *Equity 101* offers compelling evidence we can see, a framework to guide the work, and a community of learners with whom to learn. Each chapter offers descriptions of educators who are closing gaps and instituting equity in their schools. These are not composite descriptions from several schools; these are individual schools that have closed the gap and share how they achieved their goals. We engage with educators who have accomplished the task of lifting all students to high levels of success.

Curtis did not have to enter the field of education and focus on equity. Instead, he could have walked away, asserted his privilege, and denied the urgency of equity work for White people. However, while observing and interviewing and becoming part of so many classrooms' stories, he realized he could not afford to walk away, and as a result, we have *Equity 101* as a map for our journey.

None of us can afford to walk away. Our children are filling too many prisons—prisons with bars, prisons of poverty, and prisons of potential not realized. For the sake of our children, we do not have the choice to deflect the conversation. We must center ourselves in equity, and in this book, *Equity 101,* we find a path that takes us through reflection, talk, and action, all modeled on equity actualized in numerous school communities, proving it can be done.

Curtis, you may have entered education as an outsider—but now you are a respected insider. Thank you for *Equity 101.*

—*Bonnie M. Davis*

Acknowledgments

This book is only possible because of the thousands of amazing educators I have worked with over the years. Truly, you all inspire me. Your love of your students, your dedication to their success, and your willingness to accept them for who they are helped me define equity. I especially want to thank the dedicated educators of the schools featured in this book, including Northrich Elementary, Elmont Memorial High School, Rancho Verde High School, Frankford Elementary, Sanger Unified School District, Dunbar High School, and Behrman Charter Elementary. Your work continues to inspire.

Many people have profoundly impacted me and the writing of this book. Dan, you are a dream of an editor and an incredible person as well. Bonnie, you have believed in me, pushed me, challenged me, and partnered with me, and I owe this series to you. Mejkin, you provide just the writing support I need. Glenn, you brought color in to my pale life, and I am eternally grateful. Kathleen, you trust what I say which has given me the strength to push further. Dorothy, Jamie, Graig, Mike, Michael, Jenny, Jen, Rachael, Yolanda, and so many others, thank you for my education.

I also want to thank the dedicated staff at the School Improvement Network. I never thought I would have the chance to work with such creative, passionate, and dedicated people. I need to especially thank my partners in this endeavor—my parents John Linton and Blanch Linton who took out their retirement so that teachers could learn from other teachers, and my brothers Chet and Cory who are supporting me in fulfilling dreams I never imagined. Working with you is truly inspirational. I also want to acknowledge the rest of the team who put up with all I stand for: Jeff, Jeremy, DJ, Peter, Joe, Jason, Mike, Tracie, Steve, Ben, Sara, Jeannie, Amy, John, Tom, Michelle, Trent, and so many others who are making the School Improvement Network a reality.

Most of all, I want to thank my family for supporting me in writing this over weekends, on family trips, and all night long far too many times. Kids, hopefully you are too young to remember. Dear, I owe it all to you.

And, last but not least, I want to thank Jonsi for making all this bearable.

PUBLISHER'S ACKNOWLEDGMENTS

Corwin gratefully acknowledges the contributions of the following reviewers:

Pamela V. Booker, Supervisor, Office of Equity and Integration Roseville Area Schools, Roseville, MN

Isla Govan, Consultant and Facilitator, Cross Cultural Connections, LLC Renton, WA 98055

Donna Graves, Director, Equity Training and Development Montgomery County Public Schools, Rockville, MD

Josephine Jackson, Executive Director, Equity and Inclusion Duval County Public Schools, Jacksonville, FL

Dorothy J. Kelly, Retired Education Administrator Kirkwood, MO

Naomi Khalil, Director, Instructional Equity Farmington Public Schools, Farmington, MI

Dennis Lubeck, Former Director of History Programs, Cooperating School Districts St. Louis Area, MO

Tiffany S. Powell, Coordinator, Office of Diversity Manhattan-Ogden USD 383, Manhattan, KS 66502

Shawn Stibbins, Teacher Wayzata Public Schools, Wayzata, MN

About the Author

Curtis Linton is the Chief Education Officer of Curious School. A noted expert on educational equity and racism, he is the author of the Equity 101 series and co-author with Glenn Singleton of the first edition of *Courageous Conversations About Race*. As the Chief Officer of Education with School Improvement Network, he documented on film and in print hundreds of highly equitable educators and how they succeed with all kids.

With his wife Melody, he runs the Domino Foundation, which supports transracial adoption families through education and social opportunities. As a White father of two beautiful kids of Color, he considers every day the real and personal impact of racism on our students.

Prologue

This is a book about equity in education. Equity is not about equal treatment of all students. Rather, it is about equal outcomes achieved by individualizing the instruction and support for each and every child. Equity is about *all* students succeeding, especially when measured according to differences such as race, ethnicity, socioeconomic status, gender, language, family background—the list of diversities within our students goes on and on. This effort has been traditionally referenced as "closing the achievement gaps" between students from the dominant White middle-class norm and students from traditionally underserved or oppressed populations. Building equity in education shifts the focus of responsibility for academic achievement from the students to the professional administrators and teachers who are the educators in the school. Students have to do their part, but the adults in the building need to teach in a way so that all students can succeed.

Throughout this book, when I use the term *diverse* to describe students, I am referencing directly the racial and other characteristics that set apart a student from the dominant White and middle-class norms that have so defined the practices and culture of our schools. Serving one "norm" rather than the vast diversities now so apparent in today's students only guarantees the continuation of educational inequities. As educators work to directly address their school's racial and other inequities, they will accomplish equity, which is eliminating student achievement disparities and lifting all students to high levels of success.

For schools to achieve this, educators need to address equity at three levels: personal, institutional, and professional. In the first three chapters, I follow this format:

- Personally, I share my own path toward understanding equity and how it has impacted my life and work.
- Institutionally, I define what equity means for an educational institution and describe a school that achieved equity for all students.
- Professionally, I present the Equity Framework, shown as follows, which is an organizational tool that schools and school systems can use to guide their equity efforts.

Real stories of change are critically important in achieving equity. Throughout this book, I share the stories of schools, school systems, and educators who went through a change process personally, institutionally, and professionally to achieve equity for their students. These stories illustrate the process of equitizing education so that it works for all students, no matter their personal diversities.

The next three chapters go into greater depth in describing personal equity, institutional equity, and professional equity:

- *Personal equity* guides the process of centering one's self in equity and uncovering one's own biases, stereotypes, and privileges.
- *Institutional equity* explores how a school and school system can overcome institutionalized factors that limit student achievement, especially for students of Color and those from diverse backgrounds.
- *Professional equity* focuses on how efforts to successfully implement equitable practices can assure individualized support for all students.

The book ends with *moral equity:* a plea from me to you to engage honestly and sincerely in this work of educating students equitably, since their futures depend upon our own successful efforts as educators.

Throughout the book, I also prompt you to use the *equity lens* as your tool in deciphering the equity efforts of the educators in these stories—and ultimately in understanding your own efforts to equitize your work as an educator. At the end of each chapter, engage in the Equity in Action implementation exercises, which include discussion questions, reflection prompts, and implementation activities.

This book presents the Equity Framework in depth. It describes what *equity* is and what it looks like in schools. The second book, co-authored by Bonnie Davis, explores the critical topic of culture. I encourage you to begin by exploring now what *equity* is and what it looks like for you as an educator in your classroom, school, and system. Engaging this way is like understanding the weather—you can have coping strategies to deal with rain, snow, and heat, but without understanding how the weather works, you might end up trying to use a snow shovel to deal with a heat wave. By only focusing on strategies that address student needs, you will struggle to understand fully why the strategies even matter, and how they fit in the overall effort to build equity for all students.

In our collective hundred-plus year effort to succeed at educating all students, equity is now what matters. Equity is about each and every individual student achieving in our schools and learning what they need to succeed in society. Equity is a journey both for you as an educator and for the institution of which you are a part. *Equity 101* aims to engage you the reader in a journey—a journey toward eliminating racial disparity and other injustices at the personal, institutional, and professional levels. In sharing my story, I hope that you will better understand your own story and embark on a journey toward a greater understanding of equity and what it takes for all students to succeed.

Sincerely,

Curtis Linton

CHAPTER 1

Finding Equity

If *equality* guarantees equal access for students when they enter school, then *equity* guarantees equal results when students exit school. For over fifty years, equality of entrance has guaranteed that any student—Black, Brown, rich, poor—can attend the public school where they live. But troubling and persistent achievement inequity according to race, economics, and language clearly illustrate that no equality of academic success has been systemically achieved. According to DeCuir and Dixson (2004),

> In seeking *equality* rather than *equity,* the processes, structures, and ideologies that justify inequity are not addressed and dismantled. Remedies based on equality assume that citizens have the *same* opportunities and experiences. Race, and experiences based on race, are not equal. Thus, the experiences that people of color have with respect to race and racism create an unequal situation. *Equity,* however, recognizes that the playing field is *unequal* and attempts to address the inequality. (p. 29)

For far too long within our *equal* system, we have persistently failed certain groups of students who don't fit the norm of our educational system. But in a system of *equity,* all students succeed academically—especially students of Color and those from diverse backgrounds. Fundamentally, schools must change their focus from equality to equity. So, if equity is the paradigm shift educators need to embrace, then what is equity?

REALIZING EQUITY

In 2006 when I first visited Northrich Elementary, a highly diverse school just outside of downtown Dallas, Texas, I expected something special. But what I discovered was the realized ideal of modern education: *all* students performing at grade level and above regardless of race, socioeconomics, and language. No racial achievement gaps. No economic gaps. No language gaps. Yet many people thought this school couldn't be successful because the school's students were over 50 percent Latino, about 25 percent Black, over 75 percent were on free and reduced-price lunch, and about a third were English language learners. Nevertheless, the staff at Northrich had *equitably* led 100 percent of their students to grade-level proficiency and above in all subjects. For me, this represented the end of a quest to find a school that had proven it could succeed with all students. It was the first 100-percent school I had found, and I have since visited many others. For Northrich Elementary, equity became a reality.

I found myself at Northrich Elementary approximately eight months after my son's birth, thus setting the standard for what I expected in my son's education. Astounded by this highly diverse school where 100 percent of students were succeeding at grade level, my understanding of how to achieve equity began to crystallize. Equity cannot be characterized as simply a method, program, or set of standards. To quote Ed Javius of EDEquity, "Equity is not a Strategy! It is a Mind-set!" (2006, par. 1)—an expectation, a framework, a way of being, a recognition that what educators do today for students impacts them for the rest of their lives. An equitable school like Northrich has built enough internal capacity and moral purpose to successfully serve the individualized learning needs of every single student. No student is allowed to fail since all educators have personally and collectively embraced the purpose of their work: to individually support and instruct each student so that all learn what they need, when they need it, and in the way each student learns best. Truly, *no child is left behind* in an equitable institution like Northrich. But, what does it take personally for an educator to realize equity?

MY PATH TO EQUITY

Admittedly, I am not a classroom teacher. Rather, my career with the School Improvement Network took me to almost two thousand classrooms and hundreds of schools in search of the very best practices in education. Throughout these travels, I am constantly amazed at what a dedicated teacher and a focused school can accomplish with the wide range of students that occupy today's classrooms. Time and again, I have known right upon walking into a school whether or not that educational institution successfully educated all of its students, no matter who they were, what they looked like, or where they came from. I have spent many years detailing the pedagogical practices of these teachers and administrators, but I always wondered how to label the intangible beliefs, attitudes, dedication, and vision that exist within these schools. I now define this as *equity.*

My personal journey toward an ever-developing understanding of equity goes back to my very upbringing: a privileged but non-wealthy White childhood where my parents helped me understand explicitly what it takes to succeed in our society. Nothing ever required me to understand equity and diversity, and why it matters in the lives of today's students. According to the constructs I grew up with, I did what I was supposed to do, dressed in appropriate ways, stayed in school for twenty years, received a graduate degree, and began a great career. As a White male in our society, all that was left was marriage, a home, children, and traditional "hard work." With all of this, according to societal norms, my life would be considered a success, and I likely would not only maintain but also increase the comforts I always knew.

And then at age 31, I held the most beautiful little baby boy in my arms. Finally, I had a son, brought to us through adoption by a birthmother who chose us to raise this child she was inspired should be with us. I instantly placed upon him all the hopes and aspirations I had always carried. From the moment he opened his eyes and looked in my joyful and teary-eyed face, I knew that there was nothing I wouldn't do to guarantee him all the opportunities and

Equity 101—Book 1

joys he could wish for—and that had always been present in my life.

BLACK AND WHITE

But, my son is Black and I am White. Inherently, I knew I fully loved him no matter his race, but how did this beautiful Black baby in his White father's arms make things different? How might his race make his dreams different than my own—and should they even be different? Within our home and in our love, he is my son through and through, and nothing else. In society, he is Black on White—a beautiful brown-skinned boy held within peach-toned arms. My son, my boy—all my hopes and dreams embodied in a package that even I, as his father, struggle to fully understand how he is seen within our world.

The troublesome questions from others began immediately: "Is he yours?" "Where did 'he' come from?" "Is he a Katrina baby?"

Curtis Linton with his son Dominic, age 1 month

"Have you bonded with him?" Many of the comments we heard from family, friends, and strangers exposed their opinions about his race: "What a beautiful thing you have done for him!" "He is so lucky to have you!" "We're all the same in God's eyes!" Wow! My wife and I had heard that interesting things might be said to us when we, as a White couple, adopted a Black baby, but the comments and questions deeply concerned us. We now knew that we were no longer safely normed within the predictable and dominant White society we had always known. The crossroads of race was carrying out right in our very arms.

What did all this mean? "Oh, he is so tall and look at those long hands—he is going to be a basketball player." Was that meant as a racial stereotype—Black and tall equals pro sports? Or was the phrase "we are so lucky to have a child who will make us so much money [in sports]" (this was actually said) really meant as a compliment? Could what was said just have been meant as a point of conversation because the other person doesn't quite know what to say when faced with this confluence of race? Or, was the person actually sincere in the comment? Suddenly my wife Melody and I were dealing with race on a personal and immediate level that we had never before experienced, and it rattled us. All we wanted was to love our son and raise him successfully, but society demanded of us that we address his race on a daily basis—not something a White person in our society is ever expected to do.

Dominic came to symbolize for me all the work that I had done up to that point to understand race, racism, institutionalized inequities, and the need for schools to build equity for all students. My own path to equity, however, goes much further back than the birth of my son. It includes my parents, neighborhood, education, coauthoring with Glenn Singleton (2006) the book *Courageous Conversations About Race,* diverse life experiences, and the many powerful conversations I had with the best educators discussing what it takes for all kids to succeed. To center one's self in equity is not a checklist, but rather a process that involves the following:

- Understanding one's own history
- Embracing diversity
- Discovering race

- Norming difference
- Authenticating one's self in the present

The purpose of engaging in this process of centering one's self in equity is simple: if someone does not understand deeply one's own realities, it is very hard to help others—such as students—successfully negotiate their own realities.

UNDERSTANDING MY HISTORY

I grew up in a very homogenous suburb of Salt Lake City, Utah. All around me were mostly White, middle-class, Mormon households—with the exception of two families in my neighborhood: one Latino and one Polynesian. That was nearly the extent of diversity in my upbringing, other than family trips driving across the country and into Mexico where we would see—but not really get to know—people who were different from ourselves. It wasn't that my family outwardly feared or avoided diversity, we were just very naive to the experience of color and difference and ignorant to the complexities of race in U.S. society.

While growing up, similarity was the norm—the pressure was to fit in, and the rewards followed those who fit in best. All of my schooling was in Advanced Placement (AP) and honors classes, not because I was particularly intelligent, but because I so perfectly fit the norm, teachers intuitively knew how to teach me, and I knew concretely how to succeed in my community and school. The doors of opportunity were open to me and supportive hands were willingly extended. All of this led to the development of a strong belief in my own individuality and ability to succeed. Inherent to my own identity development as a White middle-class male was the confidence that comes with epitomizing the norm: if I could so easily figure out school, wasn't it likely that I would succeed throughout the rest of my life?

Critical to my own development in understanding equity was my parents' work nationally in school improvement. Without explicitly understanding that they were working toward social justice, they embarked on a twenty-year journey of changing kids' lives through improving education. My parents started the Video Journal of Education while I was still in high school. Their company had the express purpose of documenting, on video, the very best teachers and schools in North America from which they created powerful professional development materials wherein educators could learn from other educators. The company was a brainchild of my father, who was both a filmmaker and a schoolteacher. From the first day of teaching, he realized he did not know how to effectively instruct his students. With his experience in film, he envisioned placing a camera in the classrooms of the best teachers in the school and learning from them.

Several years later, he and my mother—a successful elementary school teacher—took out their retirement, bought a professional video camera, and drove across the country filming in the best schools they could find. They contacted the top experts at the time (William Glasser, Michael Fullan, Diane Gossen, William Purkey, Heidi Hayes Jacobs, and many others), filmed their workshops, and visited the schools where these experts' practices were being implemented. Firmly dedicated to the mission of improving student learning, they created video-based professional development programs based upon the work of actual educators, not just the theories.

Throughout my undergraduate and graduate college studies, I worked for the Video Journal of Education as a cameraperson and program writer. It was great work for a college student—it paid well, had flexible hours, and I traveled the country visiting schools in every state and every demographic. Even though I had no intent to work in education, as my dreams were in filmmaking, these experiences taught me two primary things: (1) there was phenomenal diversity throughout this country—diversity I neither knew nor understood, and (2) dedicated educators can accomplish amazing things with their students when applying the right practices and beliefs.

EMBRACING DIVERSITY

As I began my master's degree in fine arts in film and television production at the University of Southern California, my wife and I embraced the opportunity that Los Angeles provided us to live in a very diverse community. This was our chance to have what I once described as an "ethnic" experience. Los Angeles is a seething cauldron of difference as defined by race, language, ethnicity, and economics. It was a city wherein we as White people could choose to live among people of Color, experience their cultures, partake in the seeming exoticness of such a neighborhood, and then feel good about ourselves because we were so open-minded and accepting of the people who already lived there.

Finding an apartment in Korea Town, a part of Los Angeles that was 70 percent Latino, 20 percent Korean, and 10 percent everything else, we were now in the minority of people who looked like us. We loved the wide diversity of friendships we developed with numerous races, nationalities, and languages represented in the circle we knew. We embraced urban living and saw this time in Los Angeles as one step in our becoming progressive-minded worldwise citizens.

Only in reflection, however, have I come to understand the incredible freedom our Whiteness provided while living in downtown Los Angeles. Even though we were the racial minority in our neighborhood, we felt no limitations on where we could go or what we could do. We knew that we were only in that neighborhood for as long as we desired, and that we could just as quickly move to any other part of the city if we wished. We were blind to the fact that so many of the residents around us did not feel the same ability to embrace any corner of Los Angeles as their own.

Likewise, we felt little of the oppression and injustice people of Color so often face in the inner city: police harassment, crime, gangs, drugs, lack of opportunity, and poor schools. The main fears we faced were those our own stereotypes caused, such as being nervous around Brown and Black men we might encounter while walking back to our apartment late at night. This fear was not based on any actual experience. Rather, it originated from all the two-dimensional stereotypes that we had been fed our entire lives—stereotypes that we had never been required to challenge as unjust.

Our understanding of race and racism remained limited, however, while living in Korea Town. I called it "reverse racism" when some of the Korean apartment managers would not rent to us, despite the vacancy signs in their windows—but we still never had a problem finding great places to live. We came to embrace and love the large Latino immigrant community surrounding us, but did not fully recognize the challenges of poverty and legality they faced.

While in Los Angeles, my wife taught at Hoover Street Elementary, a school with over 2,700 students that served a vibrant but very poor community of Central American immigrants. It was one of the densest neighborhoods in the United States. Melody embraced her role as provider of opportunity and knowledge with her students. We visited students' homes, had them over to our home, and I even featured her students in my films. We loved this time of discovering the richness found within a diverse community, but we had yet to define this diversity according to race.

Getting to personally know people who so differed from us was an eye-opening experience. We saw firsthand how far the human spirit can travel despite obstacles that we had never had to face. I started to realize how much my life had provided me, even though I never grew up with much money. It was humbling to learn how the parents of Melody's students came from so little but had built so much. I might have had the prestigious graduate degree, but they were equally trying to build their dreams. Bit by bit, it became clearer that there were distinct privileges associated with my heritage (I had not yet identified it as White), even though I had never asked for such opportunity. I still clung to the belief that my success was purely based on my talents and how hard I worked even though I struggled to understand why the hard work and dreams evident in these students' families yielded different results.

Despite this growing awareness of difference in modern society, I held on to my racist proclivities. I remember always hitting the auto-lock button in my car whenever a Brown or Black man would start to cross the street in front of me, simply because they fit the stereotype of a street criminal. Eventually realizing the racist nature of this act, I decided to lock the door for anyone who crossed the road in front of me. This felt like an effective mask for my racial biases—if I could act as though I was colorblind, maybe no one would notice my racist act.

These racial judgments even landed upon those I knew and respected: Once while filming my wife's students reading "I Am" poems describing their hopes and dreams, a young Latino boy, Jose, said that he dreamed of one day being president. The thought that crossed my mind still resonates with me, "Cute Jose! What a nice little [impossible] dream."

These thoughts that raced through my mind illustrate the natural subconscious explorations of a White person figuring out the experience of race. I came ignorant and naive to racial realities—I had always been the norm and loved the exoticness inherent in color, but had never seriously questioned how society treated people differently according to race. I did not outwardly and verbally exhibit strong racist thoughts, and was disgusted by anyone who did. But I also embraced the image of success and normalcy that I had always known: a White, educated, somewhat wealthy male. I aspired to be this person, and knew very well the path I needed to follow to accomplish success as it had always been defined for me.

DISCOVERING RACE

After hearing Glenn Singleton of Pacific Educational Group deliver a keynote address, my mother approached him about appearing in a Video Journal of Education professional development program on closing racial achievement gaps. Glenn agreed, surprised that a White company from Utah was interested in producing a program featuring a Black man engaged in honest and *courageous conversation* about race in education. He knew what we did not at the time: engaging in this project would profoundly impact me, my wife, parents, and all of us at the Video Journal of Education in ways we did not foresee.

The first day we filmed Glenn, he conducted a workshop with educators in Oakland, California. From the beginning, I was caught up in what he said about race, racism, institutionalized racism, and the reality of racial inequity. Even though Glenn was explicitly talking about race, I connected to his message through my own experiences around difference—namely that of my religion. Culturally and religiously, I am Mormon.

Mormonism is one of the more misunderstood religious experiences, and I have always been highly conscious of others' misconceptions about my beliefs and culture. As Glenn talked about feeling outside the norm while he attended the University of Pennsylvania, I remembered showing up with my wife to the opening social in graduate school and being asked seriously if my "other wife" remained in Utah. This question was based upon the history of polygamy within Mormonism, even though polygamy has not been practiced within my culture for generations. When Glenn discussed having to "speak for his race" when he is the only

Black person in the room, I recalled a whole room of filmmakers looking at me to explain a misportrayal of Mormonism we had just viewed in a film. And when Glenn described not being trusted simply because of stereotypes associated with his race, I vividly remembered serving as a Mormon missionary in France and having door after door shut on me because I was seen as a member of a dubious cult.

The sense of difference I had experienced through many years of being "Mormon" were acute and always at the forefront of my consciousness when interacting with others who might not understand my heritage and me. I knew that whether or not I was a part of the religion, the culture would remain—I would always be a descendant of a peculiar people who fled to the high desert valleys of the Rocky Mountains to escape the severe persecution inflicted upon them by the majority culture of the United States. This history and identity of difference deeply resonated within me.

Slowly, however, I began to perceive a distinct difference between Glenn's sense of difference tied to his race, and my sense of difference tied to my religion. Both of us were raised well aware that individuals and society saw us as somehow different or even less than others. Both of us found ourselves confronted by negative stereotypes and limiting judgments purely based upon a two-dimensionalized view of who we were. But one thing was distinctly different between Glenn and I: not everyone knew I was Mormon, but everyone knew Glenn was Black.

NORMING DIFFERENCE

Feeling different was by no means unique to me and my heritage. The negative impacts of the *isms* of otherness: racism, heterosexism, ableism, ageism, sexism, religionism, sizeism, genderism, illegalism, classism, and many others have been well documented. In my own work and relationships, I strive to understand and respect the sense of being different and the prejudice felt by people who fall into one of these isms. Understanding the collective realities of not fitting within the norm of general society is summarized as *otherness*—the *other* is anyone who exhibits physical, cultural, and belief characteristics not shared by those in positions of power, influence, and normalcy around them.

Typically, we do not hold stereotypes and biases about those who are like us because we inherently understand them in understanding ourselves. It is only in otherness where prejudice thrives since the difference feels foreign, mysterious, and even threatening. In most all of my traits, I am the norm: White, male, educated, financially stable, heterosexual, average sized, healthy and able-bodied, and a citizen of the United States. Only within my religious affiliation and culture do I find myself outside the norm—hence the reason that my initial connection with Glenn's story of race was through my own religious experience. Despite this one difference, similarity is my norm. Consequently, I have to push myself to accept the different traits I experience in others as equal to my own traits; otherwise I revert to seeing these differences as threatening to my understanding of how society functions.

As Glenn finished the workshop, he shared how he is often approached by an educator emotionally moved by his presentation who asks the simple question, "What do I do to fix this [racism]?" His stated response was simple but profound, "Believe me." When I first heard this, I was floored. "So," I pondered, "the first thing I need to do to turn the tide of racial inequity was to simply believe this Black man when he tells of the prejudice, difference, and outright racism he has experienced?" To believe Glenn meant that I had to trust his interpretation of being followed by a clerk in a department store—it might actually be distrust of him because of his race and not an attempt at customer service. To believe him also meant that I had to accept his assertion that the police often pulled him over in his car purely because of his skin color, even though I had never experienced the same thing.

Glenn's bluntness around race was a direct challenge to two of my primary assumptions: (1) anyone could get anywhere just by working hard enough, and (2) I was not part of the U.S. societal norm because of my religious heritage. The difference with race is that skin color presents itself immediately. For me to invite prejudice based on my religion, I have to announce it to another person. But race is skin color, and racism arrives when race is present.

To understand this requires delineating between race and racism. *Race* is the common label attached to the color of one's skin based on how much melanin their skin creates, as governed by their genetics. Race is how we identify what we see in someone else. Race is Black, Brown, Red, Yellow, and even my White. Race simply is skin color, and nothing more. We are born with it, no one chooses his or her race, and the beautiful variety of race surrounds us.

Racism, however, is when we attach value to one's racial identity, whether positive or negative. Racism is a social construction that has developed over time. Racism is when we use another's skin tone—what we see—to predetermine a set of characteristics rather than letting that individual define his or her own identity. As stated earlier, people often tell me that my son will be a basketball player because he is tall and Black. Seemingly a positive affirmation of my son's trait, this is still a racist comment because it assumes that my son is something just because he looks the part. In our society, tall plus Black equals basketball player. When people label my son in this way, however, they take from him his opportunity to define himself.

Whenever necessary, I could hide my religion, but Glenn could never hide his race. The fact that I partook of privileges associated with being normed in our society had never crossed my mind, and there was power associated with this privilege— the power of never doubting my own sense of image and self-worth, freedom of choice, and always knowing that I could "make it" if I so chose. Our privilege and power allowed my wife and I to move in to Korea Town for our ethnic experience, and then move out when we wanted. My privilege and power justified me locking my car door when in the presence of racial difference "just to be safe." This privilege and power allowed me to receive a phenomenal education, unlimited opportunity, and enough family stability to pursue my dreams—and then believe it was because I alone had worked hard enough to receive the rewards.

But, if my success was no longer because of what I had done, but rather dependent upon how society treated me based upon what I looked like, then maybe I wasn't as talented and hard working as I thought I was. This realization was tough because it might also mean that those who struggled might be challenged simply because of the way society sees them. Thus, my privilege and ease in life ultimately was at the cost of those who were different from me.

Once again, I am a White father of a Black son. Could this mean that my very success comes at the expense of my own son? But

I want him to experience everything I have. As long as similarity is the norm, this is impossible. For my son to have a life unfettered by prejudice and bias, difference must be normed.

AUTHENTICATING MY PRESENT

Glenn truly changed my world. No longer could I comfortably rest within the comfort of privilege. I knew that I had to honor and fortify diversity in my own life, and in society. I had to authenticate my present by being honest about what my Whiteness and other characteristics had done for me. In being authentic, I learned how to deeply appreciate those who had assisted me personally— my parents, my teachers, and mentors. I also had to learn how to distrust the myths of dominant culture that I had lived by—myths such as "pull yourself up by your bootstraps" and other misguiding thoughts that built up my own self-worth and heritage while minimizing the contributions of others, especially people of Color.

In authenticating myself, I began to understand equity. Equity is about building the possibility for everyone to succeed, no matter what they look like or where they are from. When I first worked with Glenn, I had already visited hundreds of the best schools across the country and written numerous school improvement programs for the Video Journal of Education. I knew that the mystery of a good education for all students need not be a mystery— schools and educators everywhere were succeeding equitably with *all* students, regardless of race, ethnicity, socioeconomics, and language. The "best practices" were out there, it was only an issue of disseminating these teaching methodologies so that all educators and their students could benefit. Committing to a career with the Video Journal of Education—now known as the School Improvement Network—I focused my efforts on documenting the very best practices in education and communicating how equity for all students could be accomplished.

Three years after first working with Glenn, and only a few months after coauthoring with him *Courageous Conversations About Race* (2006), I held my son in my arms. Instantly, the negative impact of racial achievement inequities became personal for me. No longer did I have only intellectual arguments as to why the gaps were immoral. Here in my arms was the most beautiful and precious baby I could ever hope to parent, and yet, according to every statistic I had seen, he was only half as likely to succeed as a White child simply because he is Black.

But this was my child, and that was not my experience. I initially approached parenting based upon what I knew best—my own White middle-class normed upbringing. Could that work with my son? Should I just teach him all the tricks of the trade of finding success in the White world? But racism is based on skin color, and my son could not hide that. And besides, he had the most beautiful skin I had ever seen, so why would I want to hide that? He deserved every high expectation and opportunity that I had received, but some in the world would never look upon him the same way they looked upon me. If racism is based upon the values people place on a person's skin color, I now needed to consciously understand how to over-power the limiting values some might place upon my son simply because of his beautiful black skin. For my son to find *equality* in his schooling experience, I have had to define *equity,* and I invite you to do the same.

Four years later, Dominic received a sister when we adopted Maya Grace, a beautiful and deeply soulful Black girl whom we all love dearly. Despite what we have been accused of by other White people, we are not raising our children as victims of race.

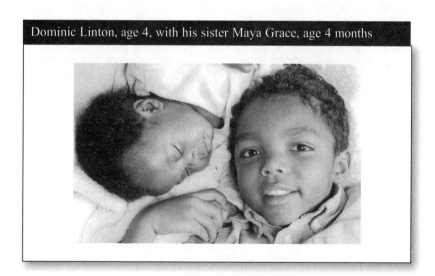

Dominic Linton, age 4, with his sister Maya Grace, age 4 months

Nor are we raising them in fear of how others may treat them simply based on how they look. My wife and I have to approach raising our children differently than we were raised, much like a school has to teach children differently who do not match the dominant norm. This is the strength of engaging personally in equity and building cultural competence. We are fortified in our knowledge of the stereotypes thrust upon our children so that we can successfully teach them how to rise above these unconscionable limitations. Engaging in equity is an effort to provide for my son, for my daughter, for Black kids, for kids of Color, for poor kids—ultimately for all kids—the opportunities, hopes, and dreams that I have always assumed for myself. Equity is about hope. Equity is about the future. Equity is about empowering our students so that after they have finished their time with us, they can self-actualize their own future success.

THE EQUITY LENS

By analyzing yourself personally, institutionally, and professionally through an *equity lens,* you can understand where you and your school need to go in order to *equitize* the schooling experience for all students.

The equity lens provided here uses the Equity Framework to guide you in examining your leadership, culture, and practice. In  doing this, you will describe yourself in terms of equity (personal), measure the equity within your system (institutional), and analyze the equitable nature of your programs and practices (professional). By applying an equity lens to yourself and your institution, you will paint a clearer picture of what you and your school need to do to achieve equity.

In *Culturally Proficient Leadership,* Raymond Terrell and Randall Lindsey (2009) say that "Change is an inside-out process in which we are students of our assumptions about self, others, and the context in which we work with others" (p. 20). They go on to describe an equity lens in the following way, "We view our work . . . as bringing us all together in the understanding that educational gaps are *our* issue" (p. 20).

The rest of this book presents several different examples of schools succeeding with all students at the elementary, secondary, and systemic levels. For each school success story, an *equity lens analysis* is provided. Within all of these schools, equity is not simply a strategy to address adequate yearly progress (AYP) and student achievement concerns; equity is about the life of the child, not just their statistical performance.

The equity lens guides us in examining the school, its educators, and how they impact students according to equity. Following is my personal equity lens, which describes the strategies I continue to use to center myself in equity. I invite you to review it, and to create your own equity lens in the Equity in Action activities that conclude this chapter.

This journey begins with us, the adults who work in education. In my experience, even though most educators support the need for attaining equity in schools, they cannot clearly define what equity is and what it looks like. Without a collective definition of educational equity, we may aim toward a worthy goal without ever actualizing it for today's students. Thus, the question arises, what is a formal definition of *educational equity?*

Figure 1.1   Equity Lens: Curtis Linton

CULTURE

Personal Strategies

- Study what it means to be White, and what it means to be of Color in our society.
- Analyze my own life in terms of Whiteness and diversity.

Institutional Strategies

- Create a collaborative environment wherein all voices are valued and supported.
- Develop institutionalized safety and respect for all diversities.

Professional Strategies

- Engage in regular conversations with people different from myself in order to build understanding.
- Represent diversity in all my work.

PRACTICE

Personal Strategies

- Challenge privilege provided to me according to my race.
- Minimize the myths of dominant culture in my interactions and ambitions.

Institutional Strategies

- Incorporate standards and practices that value diversity.
- Support development of excellence in all with whom I work.

Professional Strategies

- Differentiate support based upon needs and talents of people in my organization.
- Measure impact of equity efforts as diligently as other data analysis.

EQUITY

LEADERSHIP

Personal Strategies

- Engage with mentors and allies to guide me in my work toward equity.
- Study the work and writings of educators and other leaders who have worked to build equity in education and society.

Institutional Strategies

- Lead my organization in equitizing the work environment for all employees.
- Diversify workforce and provide opportunities for growth and success.

Professional Strategies

- Align all professional efforts so that they support the building of equity in schools.
- Engage all opportunities that provide a forum to disseminate equity principles.

EQUITY IN ACTION: CHAPTER 1, FINDING EQUITY

Equity Discussion

Describe a situation where you felt different from the dominant norm that was present. How did this impact you and your sense of safety and opportunity?

Equity Lens: Personal

On the following equity lens chart, analyze your own engagement in equity as an educator. This exercise asks you to identify in each section specific strategies that you use plus strategies that you could use to develop equitable leadership, culture, and practice. In each section, follow the prompts to identify equity-focused strategies that develop the necessary skills, understandings, attitudes, and beliefs you need to support equity. Reflect on this exercise with colleagues in your school and/or school system.

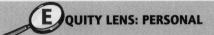

EQUITY LENS: PERSONAL

CULTURE

✓—List strategies you already use to build your own cultural competency and positive learning culture:

?—List strategies you could use to build your own cultural competency and positive learning culture:

PRACTICE

✓—List strategies you already use to deliver equitable instruction for students:

?—List strategies you could use to deliver equitable instruction for students:

EQUITY

LEADERSHIP

✓—List strategies you already use to be an effective leader of equity:

?—List strategies you could use to be an effective leader of equity:

EQUITY ACTION #1

Identify a student or someone you know who did not fit the "norm" when they went to school, but who succeeded, graduated on time, and went on to college. Preferably, this person will differ from you according to race, ethnicity, socioeconomics, and family background. Interview this person about their story and ask the following questions:

1. In what ways did you not fit the norm of your school? Describe according to race, ethnicity, culture, gender, socio-economics, language, and family background.

2. What helped you to succeed in school and beyond?

3. How would you describe the racial and other characteristics and practices of both the individuals and institutions that helped you find success?

Write a summary of your interview wherein you describe this person's equity story according to similarities and differences. Highlight in what ways this person felt different or similar from the dominant norm, and how that has impacted the individual in both schooling and career.

CHAPTER 2

Defining Equity

E quity is not about equal treatment of students, but equal educational results. With equity, all students—no exceptions—are guaranteed success in school. But, what is *equity?* What does it look like in education? And, is equity even possible? As implemented in an educational institution, I define equity as follows:

> Educators provide all students with the individual support they need to reach and exceed a common standard.

In my career with the Video Journal of Education and the School Improvement Network, I have had the unique opportunity to observe numerous *equitable* schools. It is a profoundly humbling and inspiring experience to visit a highly diverse school (as defined by a high percentage of students of Color and a high percentage of students on free and reduced-price lunch) where every student performs at grade level and above—every student, 100 percent, the whole school, every race, every economic level, every family situation, every ethnic and language background at or above grade level, year after year. These are the schools that define equity for me. Equity begins with a personal commitment to serving every student, but equity is implemented within an educational institution.

The philosophy at the School Improvement Network was always that educators learn best from other educators. This belief underlies the very purpose of this book: to define equity, illustrate it clearly, and illuminate its impact on student learning through the stories of highly successful schools and school systems that are eliminating their achievement gaps and lifting all students to high levels of success. These schools are living proof of what educators can achieve with all students, regardless of their racial identity, economic background, and learning needs. As educational institutions collectively make the paradigm shift from traditionally teaching all students *equally* regardless of differences to successfully instructing every individual student *equitably* according to each student's unique learning needs, schools can guarantee a successful education for each and every student.

Equity is about far more than test scores. Student achievement data is used to determine whether or not a school is equitable, but equity is about the whole life of the student—each student's time now in school plus the student's life and career beyond education. Keep in mind this balance between the current effort to successfully instruct each student, and the lifelong impact that this will have on the student. Who you are now as an educator determines who your students will be in the future—your students have to make the most of the opportunities presented to them, but you have to maximize the time they spend with you in your classroom, school, and school system. Equity focuses the goal of the educational institution on what matters most: the education of our students.

EQUITY SUCCESS: NORTHRICH ELEMENTARY

Northrich Elementary was the first example I personally experienced of a highly diverse school that succeeded with 100 percent of its students. As previously shared, this school defined for me what equity looks like. Just outside of Dallas, Texas, this is the poorest elementary in Richmond Independent School District (ISD). It represents the prototypical highly diverse school that has been traditionally excused from high academic achievement simply because of the type of students they serve. But at Northrich, student demographics presented an opportunity for success rather than a justification for mediocrity.

Five years prior to my visit, Sandy Nobles became the principal of Northrich. Sandy is a person at peace with the remarkable and difficult work she does in schools—she greatly respects the work of teachers and other professionals, truly loves the students, is proud of the school's accomplishments, and has a strongly reassuring presence for all who enter the school. She is a White Texas woman who leads her staff calmly but firmly toward success with all students, without exception.

Coming from the central office, she understood the school improvement initiatives put forth by the district. The school had been experiencing a significant demographic shift, and the neighborhood was struggling to embrace these changes. She entered the school wondering what would happen academically with the students if the staff fully implemented all of the "best practices" she had been working on at the district. She saw no reason why her school could not assume success for its diverse student body just as the other more wealthy and White schools in the district assumed success for their own students.

Sandy describes the work she did in the first year as a "soft sell" with her staff in gently explaining the changes that needed to happen. She observed educators in action and identified those who were natural teacher leaders and who could help her implement sustainable changes. Right up front, she also applied Jeanne Gibbs's (2006) Tribes Learning Community approach to building collaboration and support among the staff. In Tribes, the staff builds unity and trust through a series of protocols and rituals so that they rely upon each other to improve their teaching practice. Through Tribes, Sandy established consistent high expectations for students and staff along with norms of trust and communication that most of the educators had never experienced. According to Sandy, "This allowed them to quickly understand that they could trust that [this new direction was] not going to change. It was a safe place to talk together, build a sense of collaboration, and everybody would be treated fairly."

She recalls the first staff meeting she attended: teachers were spread all over the library doing their own tasks at tables. She moved staff meetings to the music room where there was enough room to put sixty-seven chairs in a circle, making everyone equal in their chance to participate and share. Meetings in a circle helped establish a culture where, according to Sandy, "We are in this together and we are going to do this together." She never handled business in a staff meeting. They began each meeting by sharing a success, a good strategy, and ways to build community in the school so that every teacher and student could have a voice each day.

The culture of the school moved from one where teachers focused on their own classroom instruction to one where they looked at data regularly and collaboratively focused on the actual work of teaching. In every meeting, teachers would reflect on what each of them was doing every day to personally improve student achievement and engagement. Tribes represented a schoolwide process for the staff that they could replicate in the classroom. Sandy explains:

> It's very important. . . . This sense of building a safe and fair place was important not only for the teachers to feel, but every student. Along the way, we really developed a sense of working together to bring all these students in the school to a place where they could learn to be successful, and it worked. It took some time, but after the first year, I really had seen the faculty pull together. We really figured out a way for critical mass to take over.

As the Northrich staff learned how to work collaboratively, the work became easier because most everyone was on board. With this engaged collaboration, they increased their focus on improving classroom teaching and learning.

Sandy and her support staff were also very intentional in how they ran team meetings:

> I really pulled grade level teams together and taught them how we were going to be *transparent*. I used that word a lot when I began. It was important for them to understand that we were going to talk about what was happening in their own classrooms with each other. We didn't do that as a whole faculty, but we did do it by grade level. We had our benchmarking and all of our other data that we could use to really look at what was going on in classrooms. That became a very transparent activity that was done regularly with myself and an instructional support teacher.

Initially, most of the teachers had never before shared their own student achievement data with team members. To build collaborative capacity, Northrich's instructional support teacher worked one-on-one with individual teachers outside of team meetings to help them understand the data the teacher was looking at and how to communicate it to team members. This additional support helped teachers feel safe in sharing their practices with colleagues.

Just like students need a teacher they can trust, teachers came to trust Northrich's instructional leaders. Sandy continues, "Building that practice and being very persistent with it really helped to build the trust. It also created enough anxiety that everyone knew that they were going to be held to high expectations. It just became the way we worked."

Visiting Northrich, I observed this trust that Sandy had developed with her teachers. They were in this effort together. The teachers clearly knew that Sandy would support them in being the absolute best that they could be. This effort on her part, however, depended on her clear communication skills. Sandy never overemphasized theory and educational jargon. When she presented new teaching methodologies and professional development to the staff, she presented it in a way that fine-tuned their current practice, rather than as theory and pedagogical concepts. She used good questioning strategies with positive presuppositions to help educators focus on their own professional growth: "Tell me about what's working in your classroom?" "Who's succeeding?" and "What's coming next?" The capacity of the school grew as Sandy and her administrative team convinced the teachers that they believed in their potential to succeed. They also removed the "surprises" from the work of school improvement by being transparent in all their initiatives and efforts. They exemplified Michael Fullan's (2010) change imperative that *capacity-building trumps judgmentalism.*

Throughout that first year, it became increasingly clear who was on board with the changes, and who was not. Sandy explains how this eventually became apparent:

Teachers that weren't pulling their weight wanted to go to a new school. Because the process had been so consistent all year, the teachers who wanted to be there and be in a school where the diversity was great and changing quickly stayed. And then others found a new school, either with my encouragement or on their own. What this allowed was for teachers to rise to the challenge. You have to be comfortable in the place, and after a year we accomplished this.

Sandy presents a critical leadership lesson in the way she worked with teachers. She discussed with those who were resistant to change how their actions were impacting student learning:

I've really learned how to separate out the personal and the facts. If I work with someone and there is some resistance, I am always going to tell them, "We are looking at data, we are looking at practice in your classroom. We are looking at the teaching and learning going on. This is about the facts. This is about the work. This is not about you." Because I filter through that this is not personal, it is about "our goals for your class and for our school," it really helps.

As Sandy directly addressed resistance among certain members of the staff while remaining transparent and honest in the process, she actually gained more trust and loyalty from the faculty as a whole. "The best thing that happened that first year in doing that with the several teachers this needed to happen with, I earned so much respect from the faculty at large because I held people accountable that the staff had been carrying for so long." According to Sandy, these actions were "respectful to the teacher, but helped the whole school."

By the second year, Northrich Elementary started to see growth in student achievement. I observed in this school an intense focus on the Texas state standards. Every classroom and every lesson had the standard that students were learning posted. Seeing this, I asked the teachers if they "were teaching to the test." The teachers provided me with a very strong response, "No, we are not teaching to the test, we are *teaching what's tested.*"

Sandy describes it as a "laser focus" on the state standards. In terms of content, the staff knew explicitly what they were supposed to teach, and students knew what they were expected to learn. But this standards focus was not simply added on to an already full curriculum. During that first year, Northrich Elementary deliberately simplified the complexity of teaching. Prior to this, teachers had to manage numerous responsibilities—pull-out programs, extra student support, noncore subject classes, and other initiatives that caused the state standards to feel like just another burdensome mandate. Working with the staff, Sandy removed all of these extra programs and allowed the teachers to focus only on teaching the standards. Teachers began to use the data and benchmarks to identify what was not working, without it being mixed up with everything else going on. The teachers responded very positively to this because it allowed them to do what is most important—teach the necessary learning every day.

In doing this, however, they had to greatly modify their traditional art, music, physical education, and other programs beneficial to student learning. Rather than continuing as stand-alone programs or expecting classroom teachers to provide this enrichment, they incorporated these opportunities—which they called "specials"—back into the rigorous standards-based learning now apparent in every class. The specials teachers would coordinate their lessons with the grade-level teachers so that the extension activities supported the standards learning. Art and music tied in to the reading and history curriculums. Physical education taught students about how healthy living impacts their success in school. Furthermore, they rearranged the schedule so that teams of teachers could collaborate while their collective students were in the specials classes.

Along with these changes, Northrich reached out to the community to bring families in to the school. They "started on the outside and then worked in" by not focusing these family nights purely on official PTA activities or parent-teacher nights. They recognized that some parents did not feel comfortable inside the school, so they held activities such as family picnics outside the building and after hours to help the community get comfortable with the staff and with the school. Well-designed community outreach efforts succeeded because the students *wanted* their families to be with them at the school. "It's paramount that everyone feel like they are part of the process. The culture building at Northrich included everyone," says Sandy.

At Northrich, the primary focus was on the success of the students. This became the culture of the school. The student achievement results manifest the wisdom of Northrich's approach, as Sandy describes:

> After four years on the state assessment, we achieved exemplary status. All of our boys and girls in all of our student groups were achieving at grade level. And we did not have an achievement gap between any of our student groups. It was a wonderful place. Our boys and girls all felt safe. They all felt like they were treated fairly. But it really came from every teacher building that sense of community in their classroom, and then therefore it was also schoolwide.

I visited and observed Northrich Elementary during the fourth year of their improvement effort. Throughout the following months as the Texas state assessment results (TAKS) arrived for each grade level, Sandy would e-mail me with an enthusiastic "100 percent!" After receiving several of these e-mails, it started to sink in what Northrich Elementary had achieved: *equity* for *all* students! So this is what *equity* looks like, I thought to myself: a staff unified in achieving guaranteed academic success for each and every individual student.

Demographically, Northrich is one of those schools that has too often been excused for not succeeding with all students: three-fourths students of Color, and three-fourths students from poverty. Even more so, Northrich is the most diverse and poorest school in the district, the one that is typically not expected to excel above all others. But they did it—no achievement gaps. They did it with every student, whether that student was Brown, Black, White, poor, middle class, English language native, or English language learner. *Every student reached grade level; every student was learning what he or she needed to succeed in this grade, the next grade, and beyond.*

After achieving 100 percent for all students, Sandy was transferred to another school. Under new leadership, Northrich hasn't lost a beat with any of its students. Reflecting upon this legacy, Sandy shares:

> The wonderful story continues about Northrich. To this day, every year on state assessment, Northrich Elementary has received exemplary status, and the student population has

stayed the same—a Title 1 school, over 70 percent qualifying for free and reduced-price lunch. That sustained academic success really shows that a school culture really can change for the better.

As I share this story of success with educators, I pose a follow-up question: Imagine if you were the teacher of the following grade or the principal of the middle school where Northrich students would attend. What would it be like to receive *all* of these highly diverse students and know every one of them is at grade level, ready to learn, with no need for remediation? This fundamentally changes how a school functions when the focus becomes accelerating every student, rather than hoping some of them might just catch up. Northrich Elementary remains a remarkable example of institutional equity that serves the educational needs of all its students.

The following chart applies an equity lens to Northrich Elementary, based on the Equity Framework. It analyzes the school's efforts at the personal, institutional, and professional levels by identifying the strategies they used to accomplish equity for all students. This is the "how" of Northrich's remarkable and equitable success.

Figure 2.1 Equity Lens: Northrich Elementary

CULTURE

Personal Strategies

- Challenge expectations and beliefs of educators in regards to Northrich's student body.
- Explore doubt and resistance among teachers.

Institutional Strategies

- Institutionalize Tribes collaboration process in school.
- Engage community to foster parental trust and support for school initiatives.

Professional Strategies

- Schedule and support teacher collaboration.
- Empower teachers to understand individual student learning needs.

PRACTICE

Personal Strategies

- Individually analyze and develop teachers' pedagogical practices.
- Expect teachers to master instructional strategies.

Institutional Strategies

- Provide professional development that models strategies across the school.
- Implement rigorous standards-based instruction.

Professional Strategies

- Provide technique for differentiating the instruction.
- Share effective pedagogical practices in teams and across grade levels.

EQUITY

LEADERSHIP

Personal Strategies

- Coach teachers individually on how to collaborate with team members.
- Support teachers when they engage in change effort, and hold accountable if resistant.

Institutional Strategies

- Simplify curriculum and schedule so teachers can focus on core instruction.
- Focus faculty meetings only on professional development.

Professional Strategies

- Provide professional development that disseminates best practices of teachers within the school.
- Provide best-practice research and strategies for staff.

EXPLORING EQUITY

Much has been written about educational equity, especially in relation to race and culture. Most of the equity literature, however, assumes that the reader has at least some experience and understanding with race, diversity, and cultural competency to help with understanding what is written. But most educators are more like me—White, middle class, and suburban—than like their highly diverse students. They may lack deep relationships and personal experience with people from different races and backgrounds than their own. Often, educators may even understand equity-related concepts intellectually, but lack personal connection to these ideas.

When I began my own work around equity, I was distinctly unprepared for the learning. Growing up in my community, I had little experience with different races. Far more powerful than the biases within me was my overwhelming ignorance of the experiences of people of Color. Before I could personally connect with the research and literature on equity, I had to address my own limitations around race and diversity.

In the first edition of *Courageous Conversations About Race,* Glenn Singleton and I explicitly present equity as it relates to race:

> Achieving true equity for all students must be a central and essential component of any attempt to close the racial achievement gap. Lacking a focus on equity, educators might experience a widening disparity in achievement among students because the root causes of the gap remain unaddressed. (Singleton & Linton, 2006, p. 46)

We go on to define educational equity as raising the achievement of all students while (1) narrowing the gaps between the highest- and lowest-performing students, and (2) eliminating the racial predictability and disproportionality of which student groups occupy the highest and lowest achievement categories (p. 46).

Despite having written about that definition, it took me many more years of observing highly successful diverse schools to actually understand it. I had intellectualized equity long before I had personalized it. Without personalizing and institutionalizing the work of equity, a leader, school, or system can claim progress toward an abstract goal of equity without ever drastically changing the policies, processes, and practices that can actually achieve equity. Because equity has been treated as a difficult, complex concept and abstractly depersonalized, it has become an ivory-tower ideal for far too many educators: *all talk, no action.*

As described in *Courageous Conversations,*

> Equity is far more than a state of being or an abstract ideal. Rather, it is an operational principle that enables educators to provide whatever level of support is needed to whichever students require it. In the classroom, this means providing each and every student with what each individually needs to learn and succeed . . . [Equity] assures that *all* students will have the opportunity and support to succeed. In an equitable system, the barriers that inhibit student progress are removed. Students of Color and their families can rest assured that the school will meet their needs to the same degree it meets White students' needs. Equity does not mean that every student receives an equal level of resources and support toward his or her educational goals. Rather, equity means that the students of greatest need receive the greatest level of support to guarantee academic success. (p. 47)

DESCRIBING EQUITY

Numerous definitions of equity have been used in education. Most respect the diversity of students, and many are tied to equality in treatment. When working with groups of educators, I often pose the question, what is equity? Typical responses include:

- Treating all kids fairly and equally.
- Respecting the cultural backgrounds of all students.
- Helping all students reach their highest potential.
- Making sure no students fail.
- Equality of access and opportunity.
- Teaching students according to their own learning needs.
- Providing students with what they need to succeed in society.
- Understanding the desires of students' parents and community.
- Respecting differences.

Rarely do I hear the same explanation of equity—a hundred educators, a hundred definitions. Consequently, there remains a great lack of common understanding about equity. Without a consistent definition of equity, a school or system addressing its educational inequities while it tries to "close the gaps" may actually discover educators are working toward different objectives. Without unity of understanding around equity, educators are not likely to achieve unity in effort.

When looking at formal definitions of equity (Equity 2010), they tend to fall into three categories:

1. Justice, fairness, and freedom from bias or favoritism.

2. Legal and procedural rules and documents that serve to protect rights and enforce laws.

3. Rights, claims, and ownership interests, especially as it relates to stocks and businesses.

Factoring these three categories into education establishes equity as foundational to systemic success for all students:

1. Fairness and justice in education are established for all students so that none are subject to prejudiced bias or favoritism.

2. Institutional policies, rules, and practices are established that guarantee access to educational opportunity and success for all students.

3. With an equitable education, students *own* their posteducation success and opportunities—in a sense, they own stock in their personal futures.

Defining equity need not be complex and convoluted. True educational equity will impact who we are, what we do, and how we do it in a practical ground-level way so that real success can happen for all students, no matter who they are or where they come from. Applying this to my own schooling experience, it's obvious that I unequally benefited from my school's *inequities.* My own education—small classes, honors and AP track, veteran teachers, interesting learning, high expectations, and ultimately a full-ride scholarship to college—worked very well for me, but was not always the typical experience of my classmates.

My high school was organized in an "equal" fashion where all students received the same instructional time each day, regardless of student demographics or learning readiness. But, this supposed "equality" was inherently inequitable—the system worked *unequally* to my advantage in giving me more time and resources than I needed at the expense of less fortunate students. The institution showed inherent bias to those of us who "fit the norm" and naturally connected with school. From kindergarten through twelfth grade, I was mostly with the same group of "honors" students. We were tracked in this matter not because of any special skills or gifts, but because we were well liked by our teachers, the best behaved, and most likely to succeed according to the norms of our community. Consequently, we had the best teachers—always. We had the highest expectations—always. We were provided unfair opportunities and support that few students received. We also all went on to college and began successful careers at a far greater rate than most of my more diverse classmates.

The common characteristic among my successful cohorts was how well we fit the school's norm. Much later in life I realized how few of my classmates outside of my honors track had received the same education. I might have played football with them, but rarely did we share an academic class. The *equal* approach to education that my school system traditionally embraced lead it to be an *inequitable* experience for far too many students.

EQUITY DEFINITION

In contrast to my own schooling experience, I have observed dozens of equitable schools in my career with the Video Journal of Education and School Improvement Network. Northrich Elementary, Sanger Unified School District, Dunbar High, Frankford Elementary, Elmont Memorial High, Behrman Charter Elementary, and others described in this book exemplify the principles and reality of equity. All of these schools evaluated who they were and why they existed, and then changed their practice so that all students could succeed academically. Visiting these schools in person, I am constantly in awe at the possibility they represent: *every student succeeding every day regardless of who they are or where they come from.* These schools represent not only the best in education, but the very ideals of a free and prosperous democratic world where truly anyone can engage in "life, liberty, and the pursuit of happiness." What if *equity* achieves *equality* for all?

Describing Frankford Elementary's journey to equity, the principal Sharon Brittingham describes the instructional reality when she first arrived at the school in Frankford, Delaware. "When I came here the teachers really did believe that they were doing the best job for the population that they worked with. But what had to change was that belief that these children could learn at high levels of expectations." These teachers worked hard and cared for their students, who were equally Black, White, and Latino, three-fourths from poverty, and one-third English language learners. The culture of the school had collectively accepted, however, a lower level of achievement for their students—despite their caring, they came to believe that their students were not capable of performing at the same level as other students in Delaware. Seven years later, after changing their expectations, examining their beliefs, and equitably focusing on each and every student, the staff at Frankford Elementary became one of the highest-performing schools in Delaware with well over 90 percent of all students at grade level in all subject areas and an astounding 100 percent grade level achievement in reading and science.

At Amherst Middle School in Amherst, Massachusetts, equity-minded principal Mary Cavalier describes the school's instructional approach as, "by developing curriculum that works for every kid and teaching that curriculum in a way that works for every kid, we are providing an *equitable* education for every child in this building." With equity, every student succeeds because every student receives support in the way they need.

The common trait found within these highly successful diverse schools is that they have operationalized equity. Equity is not simply a belief, an ideal, or an abstract concept. It is an actualized reality lived every day. But what lacked was a common definition to define what these educators were doing. School after school that I visited described their practice along the lines of *individually teaching each student according to their needs so that every student could reach an acceptable level of performance.* After observing dozens of these schools succeeding with all students, a practical definition of educational equity began to materialize.

There are many definitions of equity in the academic and professional development literature, but few of them give much guidance to educators in terms of their day-to-day work within a school. Based upon these highly successful diverse schools, I developed the following definition for educational equity:

> Educators provide all students with the individual support they need to reach and exceed a common standard.

In an equitable school, policy plus practice dictates that the educators meet the needs of each student to ensure that every student reaches an acceptable level of proficiency, regardless of that student's diversity. Equity as a foundational principle of schooling guarantees that every student has what is necessary to succeed while in school *and* after graduation—equity removes schooling as one of the barriers people face in their lifelong quest for happiness and success. When a child has received a successful education, the individual gains control of his or her future destiny. Is any child not deserving of this? Equity is the paradigm shift necessary for educators to embrace in order to fulfill the fundamental promise of education: that *all* kids learn what they need to not just survive but thrive within our rapidly changing world.

DECONSTRUCTING EQUITY

Deconstructing this definition of educational equity illustrates why equity fundamentally shifts the paradigm for educators and school systems:

Educators provide . . .

Policy, practice, and beliefs dictate that the administrators and teachers within a school and school system primarily accomplish equity. The responsibility to guarantee the academic success of all students relies first and foremost upon the professionals who work in the educational institution. Other stakeholders, such as parents, the community, and the legislature, impact this effort but the educators exercise ownership of student success.

All students . . .

Policy, practice, and beliefs in an equitable school dictate that *every* student is served and taught uniquely and fairly, regardless of the student's race, gender, socioeconomic status, ethnicity, culture, language background, family and home life, learning needs, and whether or not the student fits the norm of the school or the teachers. In an equitable school, *no* single student is left unserved, no matter the student's situation or needs.

With the individual support they need . . .

Policy, practice, and beliefs in an equitable school dictate that *every* student is sufficiently taught and supported according to the student's individual learning needs. An equitable school embraces difference and diversity as the norm, and thus recognizes that no two students are alike in their needs, background, readiness level, or learning styles, and thus no two students can be taught and supported exactly the same way all the time.

To reach and exceed . . .

Policy, practice, and beliefs in an equitable school dictate that *every* student not only reaches grade-level performance, but potentially exceeds it. Equity does not force students to an equal outcome, but guarantees that they all learn enough to achieve an acceptable outcome. Once every student is at least at grade level, the school's ability to lift *all* students far beyond this grows exponentially. As resources are no longer spent on remediation, they are applied to the *acceleration* of all students, regardless of who they are or where they come from.

A common standard . . .

Policy, practice, and beliefs in an equitable school embrace a common measurement or standard to determine whether or not each student has reached an acceptably minimal level of performance. Without the school's embrace of a common standard—typically established district, state, and national learning standards such as the Common Core State Standards—inequities will persist because one student's lower performance and one student's higher performance are both deemed acceptable just because of who the students are and where they come from. As educators within a school apply a common measurement and performance standard to all students, they can accurately measure not only what a student has learned, but what the student still needs to learn.

In a school that functions according to this definition of equity, the focus is on the possibilities of the student rather than his or her limitations. Bonnie Davis (2006) writes, "To assign an assumption to any child at any level can be dangerous" (p. 25). In applying these equitable principles, students redefine their own capabilities for success. Equity is moving students upward and forward to much greater heights of academic success than they might have thought possible. Equity is guaranteeing that all students not only have the opportunity to access a good education, but that they succeed at it. Equity works for each and every student's race, ethnicity, background, gender, and socioeconomic status.

But equity success depends on three critical elements: the educator's *personal connection* with this work, the *institution's* embrace of systemic change and progress, and the *professional practices* the teachers and administrators implement every day. As educators connect personally and institutionally with this work, they will find themselves within the right context as professionals to actualize educational equity:

Educators provide all students with the individual support they need to reach and exceed a common standard.

EQUITY IN ACTION: CHAPTER 2, DEFINING EQUITY

Equity Discussion

As a group, discuss the definition of equity presented here:

Educators provide all students with the individual support they need to reach and exceed a common standard.

In what ways do you agree or disagree with this definition? How can this definition of equity be operationalized in your school and/or school system?

Equity Lens: Institutional

On the following equity lens chart, analyze your educational institution's support of equity in your classroom, school, and/or school system. This exercise asks you to identify in each section specific strategies your institution currently uses, plus strategies that your institution could use to develop equitable leadership, culture, and practice. In each section, follow the prompts to identify equity-focused strategies that drive the skills, programs, instruction, and initiatives in your school and/or school system necessary for equity to occur. Reflect on this exercise with colleagues in your school and/or school system.

EQUITY LENS: INSTITUTIONAL

CULTURE

✓—List strategies your institution already use to build cultural competency and a positive learning culture:

?—List strategies your institution could use to build cultural competency and a positive learning culture:

PRACTICE

✓—List strategies your institution already use to deliver equitable instruction for students:

?—List strategies your institution could use to deliver equitable instruction for students:

EQUITY

LEADERSHIP

✓—List strategies your institution already use to develop effective leaders of equity:

?—List strategies your institution could use to develop effective leaders of equity:

EQUITY ACTION #2

Within your school and/or system, convene a formal discussion to establish your own institution's definition of educational equity. Assure that this collective definition individualizes student support and leads *all* students to acceptably high performance.

CHAPTER 3

Framing Equity

I n a traditional *equalized* school, equality is guaranteed at the entrance: all students have an equal chance to enter the school each day; an equal chance to participate in the fixed number of subjects, periods, and learning opportunities; and an equal chance to access the school's learning resources. *Brown v. Board of Education* guaranteed access for all students to enter the school, but it never addressed what actually happens professionally in the school to support the learning of all students. Since we live in an unequal world, students coming from diverse backgrounds and widely divergent racial, cultural, ethnic, economic, language, gender, and educational backgrounds may need different instructional support than the supposed equalized treatment that so many schools traditionally provide.

After observing veteran teachers struggling with a changing student body, Gary Howard (1999) shares the question that was posed to him: "Why are they sending these kids to us?" (p. 2). He then states that diversity within the student body is our reality: "Diversity is not a choice, but our responses to it certainly are" (p. 2). In today's workforce, students no longer have the luxury of graduating simply because they made it to the end of twelfth grade. They need skills and understandings that can be applied in their life after school. With so much diversity in today's schools—even among White students, teachers can no longer teach all students in similar ways.

A distinct challenge exists, however, for the adults teaching and administrating within the building. Since school almost always worked well for most professional educators when they were students, they readily assume that schools are naturally set up to work well for all students. They become professional educators believing that schools inherently support and value all students for who they are. Consequently, professional educators struggle to understand the unequal results of our equalized modern school system. *If school worked for me, why doesn't it work for my students?* The challenge in today's schools is diversifying the learning experience so that it works first and foremost for the students, not just the adults in the building.

EQUITY SUCCESS: ELMONT MEMORIAL HIGH SCHOOL

About the same time I first observed Northrich Elementary in Texas, I documented the work of the teacher who had the highest passing rate of African American students in the country on the AP World History Exam—an example well-worth studying to help define educational equity. Mike Indovino, "Indo" to his students, is a White, stocky, male teacher with broad shoulders, a tough face, and strong New York accent. He teaches at Elmont Memorial High School just outside of Queens, New York. Since Advanced Placement teachers and classes have historically struggled to meet the learning needs of Brown and Black students, my curiosity drove me and my team to ask: who was this man whose teaching practice worked so well for Black students?

Describing how he relates to students, Mike says, "I always play a game with them the first time they [the students] meet me. I'm mean; I'm nasty; I'm gruff, deep, horrible voice—the look alone, forget about it, right? And I tell them, I'm the best there is." The Elmont Memorial student body is 75 percent Black, 12 percent Latino, and 24 percent low income. Situated in a working-class neighborhood, it is the most diverse school in the district and assumed to be the "toughest" school to work at for staff members. But the staff at Elmont Memorial has found a formula for success with over 90 percent of its senior students scoring proficient or above on the New York State Regents Exam, with no statistical racial or economic achievement disparities.

Mike exemplifies the passion and dedication typical of the educators at Elmont Memorial High. Before students ever enter his class, they have learned of the high expectations he has for them. Mike meets his upcoming ninth grade when they are in eighth grade, during the last week of school, to assign summer homework. At this time, students receive the first nine chapters of work with the understanding that the work for the first two chapters is due the first day of school. In his classroom, rigor is always apparent: "I told them that they need to be two chapters ahead of me throughout the year." Students are expected to research the discussion questions through the textbook, Internet, and multiple other resources. Every day in class, Mike conducts a highly engaged conversation around these discussion questions.

Daily preparation on the part of the students is essential. As described by Mike, "The first day I come not prepared to teach, you [the student] can come not prepared to learn. The first day I come without a pen or pencil, so can you. The first day I come late, so can you." This preparation pays off in terms of student achievement. "They all have their discussion questions. And I tell them, 'If you don't have it, you don't come to class. Wait outside because you are not prepared to learn.' And yet, have I had to throw anyone out this year? No."

This works because of the trust that develops between Mike and his students. It is not a relationship simply defined by friendship, but rather of expectation and success. In the classroom, he distinctly expects his students to respond to the rigorous curriculum he presents, and his students know that he only has their best interests in mind. Mike treats his ninth- and tenth-grade students with respect, both intellectual and personally:

> How do you define respect? When I speak you listen. And when you speak, I'll listen. . . . My job is to make things clear to you. So if you don't understand, you have to question me. You have to let me do my job. And, if you don't understand, I'll do it again. There is no such thing as a stupid question. Kids want to learn. Kids don't want to fail. Kids want to succeed. And they want to be given the tools to succeed.

Mike overtly trusts the students' abilities to engage deeply with him in the lesson—and he has the skills to teach them in an engaging, even entertaining way.

According to Elmont's students, they clearly know what leads them to success, both in Mike's class and throughout the school:

- "When [teachers] are teaching, their love for what they do comes across. You have to love what you do before you try to teach it to someone else."
- "It makes the material interesting. It makes you want to learn all the time."
- "If teachers know what they are talking about, they are sure of it. If you have a question, and they can answer it no matter what, then you are into that lesson."
- "The teachers have high expectations. They know that we are going to excel, that we are going to live up to it."

Elmont Memorial High School did not always experience this level of success. Principal John Capozzi describes how the staff began a discussion several years ago wherein they determined that their current efforts were not sufficient for the students' needs. Traditionally, the school considered it a success for students to simply pass the New York State Regents Exam, with no worry about actual proficiency levels. Posing the question collectively, "Why are we teaching kids only to pass? Why can't our kids achieve mastery, which is 85 percent on the New York State Regents Exam," the staff embarked on a journey of excellence and equity for all of their students.

The students are the beneficiaries of this focus on excellence, and they communicate this clearly with their teachers through their willingness to engage and be pushed academically. At the end of ninth grade, Mike passes out letters to those students who he feels are ready to succeed with the increased rigor of AP world history in tenth grade. Reflecting on the previous year, he shares:

I handed out about fifty letters. The other kids who didn't get letters, all but one, came to me and said, "What do I have to do? Show me what I need to do and I will show you in the next marking period." And I tell them, "Go for it. If you can, this is what I need to see you do. If you can do it, God bless you!"

With Mike's lead, his students take ownership of their academic success, resulting annually in the highest passing rate nationally of African American students on the AP World History Exam.

The results achieved by this dedication to students at Elmont Memorial High School speak loudly: Over 99 percent of the incoming ninth graders consistently graduate from high school. Of these, at least 94 percent continue on to college. Elmont truly is an equitable school in providing each of its students with high expectations, rigor in the classroom, relevancy to their own lives, and meaningful relationships with teachers and staff. Even more important, Elmont is equitable because it deliberately provides students with what they need, both now in school and in their posteducation future.

Reflecting on his role as a teacher, Mike points to the wall behind him covered with dozens of student photos. "They come back and visit after they go to college. I'm invited to weddings. I'm invited to sweet sixteens. I'm lighting candles." At this moment, "Indo" pauses in reflection of what he has accomplished with his students. "As a teacher, kids have to know that you actually care," he says. "Kids have to see that you are the best that you can be."

Figure 3.1   Equity Lens: Elmont Memorial High School

CULTURE

Personal Strategies

- Facilitate strong culture of teacher excellence and support.
- Challenge traditional beliefs in ability of student groups to learn at high levels.

Institutional Strategies

- Celebrate high performance of school in all areas.
- Create college-bound high-achieving academic culture.

Professional Strategies

- Teach every student and every class as though they are AP or honors level.
- Let students own learning and show respect for student interpretation of curriculum.

PRACTICE

Personal Strategies

- Develop high expectations of teacher efficacy.
- Require content expertise to facilitate student discussion.

Institutional Strategies

- Practice teaching methods such as Socratic seminars that require student engagement.
- Place strong emphasis on teaching standards and college readiness.

Professional Strategies

- Use high-yield strategies in classroom instruction.
- Provide clear learning expectations for students, including homework and goals of curriculum.

EQUITY

LEADERSHIP

Personal Strategies

- Stress teachers' high dedication to success of every single student.
- Empower educators to lead instructional improvements with team and individually.

Institutional Strategies

- Strongly focus whole school on annual performance targets.
- Create and uphold powerful vision year after year to clarify the direction of the school for all.

Professional Strategies

- Hold all administrators and teachers accountable for academic performance of all students.
- Support vertical instruction across grades.

FRAMEWORK VERSUS STRATEGY

This book is deliberately designed for the adults who work in today's schools. It addresses the necessary beliefs, expectations, and foundations educators need to guarantee that all students will succeed, rather than simply hoping that the students will eventually conform to the teaching habits of the adults. This book embraces a *framework* rather than a *strategy* approach. For too long, school improvement efforts have been narrowly focused on finding the "right strategy" without addressing the context within a school necessary for the strategy to succeed. The success of equity depends on the school and/or system's ability to create an effective framework that guides all decisions, practices, and policies according to equity. Most educational institutions engage numerous strategies, but an *equitable framework* links these strategies together in order to provide guiding and driving purpose to the school's improvement efforts.

Figure 3.2   An effective framework organizes the different strategies that lead to a goal

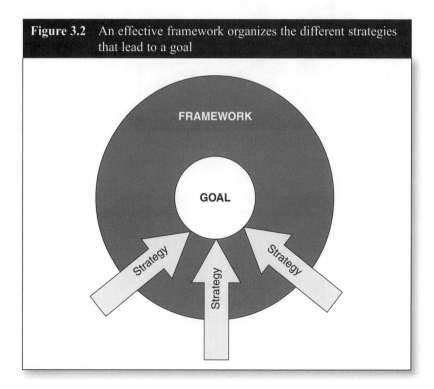

As illustrated here, a *framework* ties together various strategies and focuses them on a common goal. Without a guiding framework, individual strategies primarily serve their own purpose regardless of what else is happening, and may even work against each other. A curriculum strategy only serves to improve the curriculum. A collaboration strategy only serves to build collaboration. But what is the goal of both these strategies in the larger context of school improvement?

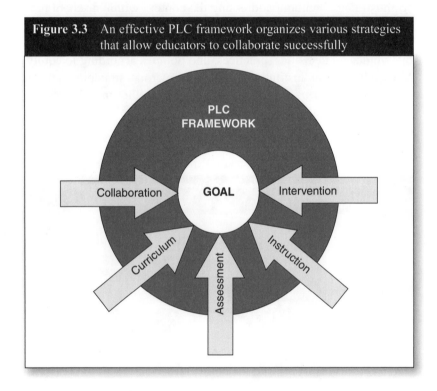

Figure 3.3   An effective PLC framework organizes various strategies that allow educators to collaborate successfully

Professional Learning Communities (PLCs) are a great example of an effective framework that pulls together various strategies dealing with collaboration, curriculum, assessment, instruction, and intervention. These are all effective strategies on their own, but collectively they are far more effective when held within the PLC framework. Without a clear framework, few of these strategies can drive sustainable success like a well-functioning PLC.

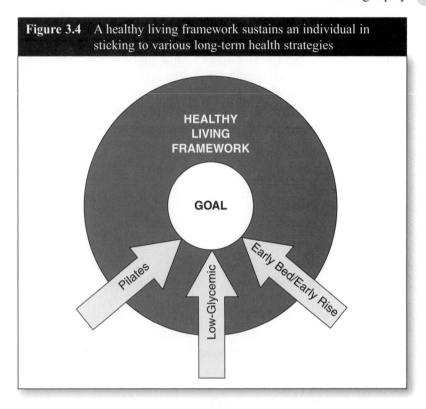

Figure 3.4 A healthy living framework sustains an individual in sticking to various long-term health strategies

The analogy of a healthy lifestyle illustrates the difference between a framework and strategy approach. When an individual embraces a framework of healthy living, this person creates lifelong habits of healthy eating, regular exercise, and treating the body well. Within this, the individual might engage certain strategies such as Pilates training, a low-glycemic diet, and an early-to-bed/early-to-rise sleep regimen. Each of these strategies is well integrated into the individual's framework of healthy living. Conversely, if an individual only focuses on the strategies of healthy living devoid of any overriding framework, then the individual is prone to yo-yo dieting and sporadic exercise efforts. For instance, the individual might engage the strategy of the high protein diet, lose substantial weight, but then regain the weight once the diet strategy has ended. Without a framework in place, the individual exerts significant effort with few long-term effects. By first embracing an effective framework before the strategies, the individual expends the same amount of energy to create lifelong successful habits.

Historically within education, "closing the gap" strategies have little lasting impact because the framework defining why the work matters is never clearly articulated. Thus, eliminating "the gaps" remains an idealistic yet seemingly unattainable goal populated with well-meaning but unconnected strategies. By applying a framework to equity—the Equity Framework—a school addresses its context, builds understanding of the students, and creates a powerful learning culture that guides the effective implementation of best-practice strategies. The Equity Framework provides meaning and guidance to the critical work of succeeding with all students, no matter their race, socioeconomic situation, or background.

THE EQUITY FRAMEWORK

After workshops on equity and closing racial achievement gaps, I am often approached by an educator who will ask me, "Do you think *it* can actually be done?" I always find this question particularly disturbing since it suggests that the educator asking the question doubts whether all students can actually achieve at comparably high levels. Without the educator's belief in this possibility of all students achieving, can it really occur? This doubt contradicts what I have personally observed in numerous schools and classrooms—the reality of schools eliminating their achievement inequities and lifting all students to at least grade-level performance and above.

In response to the doubts of these educators, my colleagues and I at the School Improvement Network produced a video series titled *No Excuses! How to Increase Minority Student Achievement.* The sole purpose of this program was to clearly illustrate schools that have eliminated their achievement inequities. So often, educators are asked to implement a change that they have never actually seen in practice. By producing a video series that provided proof as to how schools eliminate their academic inequities, we believed we could turn educators' doubts into beliefs about their students' potential to achieve. After all, seeing is believing.

We identified eight elementary and secondary schools across the country that had either fully or substantially closed their achievement gaps, and had the data to prove it. We were not quite sure what we would find, other than proof of success. I traveled with my film crew to document the practices, programs, and organization of these schools. At each site, we conducted extensive interviews with the school leader and the school's most successful teachers. We learned about the school's history, its learning culture for both adults and students, relationships with the community, the educators' individual and collective beliefs and feelings, and the pedagogical practices and strategies used within the school. Our hope was that through this project we could show educators how to change their own schools based upon the way other schools have succeeded with all students.

Despite unique and localized practices, certain trends strongly emerged in school after school that we visited. These trends correlated with what we had documented over many years in previous work at other highly successful schools. These commonalities form the basis of the Equity Framework, as illustrated here, which is a framework-style guide to what schools need to do to close and eliminate achievement inequities—and guarantee the success of all students—regardless of race, socioeconomics, ethnicity, gender, and language.

The first and most prominent trend among these schools was that equity formed the foundation of everything they did—equity for all students was the goal and central purpose of these schools. Hence, equity is placed at the center of this framework. These educators did not always use the term *equity,* but the concept, beliefs, and practices were the same.

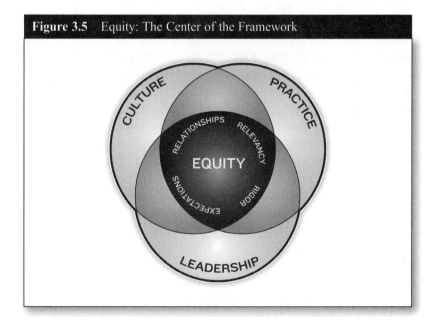

Figure 3.5   Equity: The Center of the Framework

EQUITY FRAMEWORK: CHARACTERISTICS

Within these equitable schools, we also observed four common characteristics of equity: (1) expectations, (2) rigor, (3) relevancy, and (4) relationships. As *equity characteristics,* they circle equity symbolizing that without these four characteristics present for all students no matter their diversity, other school improvement efforts may struggle to succeed. These four characteristics are key to accomplishing equity. If any one of these equity characteristics is missing from an individual student's experience in school, that student is likely *not* to succeed:

1. *Expectations* set the bar for high achievement.
2. *Rigor* provides the skills and learning the student needs to succeed.
3. *Relevancy* connects the learner with the instruction and curriculum.
4. *Relationships* help the student believe in the teacher's high expectations, engage with the rigorous curriculum, and respond to the relevancy of the learning.

These four characteristics are key to the ongoing and successful efforts of any equity-minded school.

I observed this vividly at Rancho Verde High School in Moreno Valley, California. Scott Scambray had been principal for several years at this very diverse high school, with 85 percent students of Color and over half the student body on free and reduced-price lunch. While increasing support at Rancho Verde for the lowest-performing students, Scott also focused the teachers on accelerating the students who were aiming to graduate, but not on a college-prep track. Typically, these students maintained a C average and focused on finishing high school—often the first in their family—but were unaware of the preparation and focus needed to attend college. These students rarely failed a class, but rarely excelled either. They maintained GPAs sufficient for participation in extracurricular activities and sports, but struggled in personal study skills and balancing academics with work and social activities. These were the students the school equitably believed could rise to much higher levels of achievement with the proper support.

Once a teacher identified one of these students in the ninth or tenth grade, the student was referred to the principal. In this meeting, the principal informed the student that he or she was being placed in a combined college-prep world literature/AP world history class. These students were not given the option of choosing whether or not they wanted to be in this class—they were told that they had the potential to succeed in this more rigorous college-prep track, and that they would be strongly supported along the way. The principal let the students know that if they ever had a problem with the class, they needed to speak to him directly.

In doing this, Rancho Verde exemplified the four equity characteristics. The school communicated the high expectations they had that the student could do more. The student was placed in a rigorous classroom that would challenge his or her learning. The curriculum was designed to be relevant for the diversity of students who attended the school. Finally, the teachers were highly effective at building strong relationships with each and every student.

Exemplary teachers Jeff Odien and John Black teach the combined college-prep world literature/AP world history class during the tenth grade. Together, they have created a very supportive learning environment for students. They focus on connecting students personally with the literature and making world history relevant to their lives. As described by Jeff, "They don't care what you know until they know that you care. One thing we try to make clear from day one is that we do care about them. We do care about their success and what happens with them."

In a lesson I observed, the students engaged interactively after having read *All Quiet on the Western Front*. They sat on the ground between their rows of desks to symbolize the trenches World War I soldiers lived in. Through the use of video, slides, quotes, illustrations, and stories, Jeff and John vividly illustrated what life was like for the World War I soldiers. They saw photos of "trench foot" and gruesome injuries, studied death statistics, and listened to the words of actual soldiers who had survived. For a culminating assignment, students wrote powerful "letters home" as if they were actually soldiers in the trenches:

Dear Mama,

Months have gone by since I left home and I'm sorry for not writing as much as I should. Through the months, I have seen more dead bodies than food rations. The sleep that remains unslept is replaced by the constant fear of bullets flying past my face. The gas I constantly imagine I am breathing in. If only water, fresh water, could be rationed more often. My throat no longer feels like a throat. Comrades of mine have suffered from trench foot, the feet blackened with no feeling, the overall size of the foot is horrifying. The pain that can come from this can be heard in the dead of night: men weeping and wailing, the strength drained from the most powerful men. My love for you is how I live.

The particular female student of Color who wrote the preceding letter connected to the rigor of the class, the high expectations placed upon her by the school, the relevancy of history that has become personalized, and the trust developed by her relationship with the teachers. She now sees her own potential as a learner and scholar— a potential she may have never felt before.

As described by one of the students in this class, "We have a really high standard in here, and we get used to that standard. So, in any class that we take from now on, whether it is going to be another AP class or a regular class, we are going to treat it as if it is an AP class." These students, placed by the principal in this accelerated program, are supported in all of their academic endeavors through college-preparatory programs like Advancement Via Individual Determination (AVID).

"The truth is everybody here has similar expectations," explains Fred Workman, superintendent of Val Verde Unified. "We believe children can learn and we believe in our motto 'no excuses.' At the end of an instructional period there should be progress." This *no-excuses* attitude led to significant equity progress at Rancho Verde High School. During the time that he was principal, Scott Scambray placed over 750 students in this accelerated program. These were students who previously had only seen themselves as worthy of high school graduation, but now hundreds of students see themselves as capable of college and success beyond.

Within these highly successful schools that exhibited the equity characteristics, we likewise observed time and again that the strategies they used to accomplish equity could be organized according to leadership, culture, and practice. The key to the schools' success was the balance they exhibited between these three strategic areas in professional development and support. These schools had developed their own frameworks that allowed them to align and synergize all of their improvement strategies. They put forth equal effort to develop leadership, build a successful school culture, and implement best practices in classroom instruction and student support.

When I poll educators in workshops, most say they spend at least 80 percent of their school improvement efforts on practice— specifically, the pedagogical practices of teachers in the classroom.

This leaves very little time, energy, and resources to build strong leadership and develop equitable culture and cultural competency among the staff. Today's typical school is thus unbalanced in its improvement efforts—an imbalance that comes from pursuing a strategies approach with no guiding framework. The constant barrage of new and unrelated strategies leads to the continual frustration of many educators with professional development since nothing seems focused when school improvement efforts have no clear direction.

In the highly successful schools we have studied and documented, we found a deliberate effort to balance their professional development, school support, and improvement strategies with respect to leadership, culture, and practice. These schools have applied a framework approach to all of their improvement efforts—they have answered who they are and what their goals are for their students, and aligned all strategies accordingly.

THE EQUITY FRAMEWORK: LEADERSHIP

The leadership strategies of the Equity Framework address district, principal, and teacher leadership needs. According to Kati Haycock, director of the Educational Trust, "Focus on the things you can control and not the things you can't. . . . The leader is key in all of this— it's about coherence, focus, relentlessness" (as cited in Video Journal of Education [VJE], 2006). Equitable leadership organizes strategies that build vision and direction, drive accountability, sustain innovation, and support systemic equity:

- Strong vision and direction focus on the goals that address both student learning and teacher performance, along with the roles of all stakeholders in the school. Strategies that build vision and provide direction place the school or system succinctly on a path toward success.
- Educator accountability addresses the high expectations placed on teachers and school leaders, the support they receive to reach these expectations, and the efforts of the school or system to hold them responsible when they fall short. When strong accountability becomes institutionalized, schools refocus their priorities and decisions on the needs of the students, and not the demands of adults within the building.

Figure 3.6 The Equity Framework: Leadership

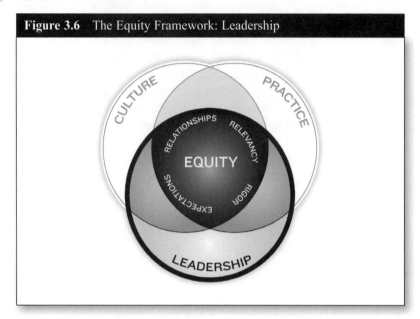

- To sustain innovation, schools develop and deliver professional development that is timely and critical for the teacher's success. Professional learning needs to be both job embedded and designed to build capacity among the teaching corps. This occurs when staff development strategies focus on implementation and teachers are supported through coaching, collaboration, and on-demand instructional support.
- As a school or district institutionalizes systemic equity, the leadership can focus on a simple formula:

Building equity =
understanding difference + access & opportunity + social justice

When building systemic equity, educational leaders embrace strategies that build *understanding of difference*—such as fostering effective, safe, and honest communication through *Courageous Conversation About Race;* guaranteeing *access and opportunity* so that all students receive an honest chance for success during and after their education; and empowering stakeholders with *social justice* strategies that help educators and students realize their own potential for success.

THE EQUITY FRAMEWORK: CULTURE

In the Equity Framework, the strategies that build culture focus on both the *learning culture* of the school and on the *cultural competency* of its educators. With a strong learning culture, the school becomes a place where teacher, leader, and student alike feel supported to take risks, stretch, and learn without fear of failure. As educators become culturally competent, they first learn about themselves—who they are racially, culturally, and ethnically, and what biases, beliefs, judgments, and expectations they carry, especially toward those students who differ from the norm; and then they come to understand all of their students—both individually and grouped—according to race, culture, ethnicity, background, learning needs, and in what ways they fit or do not fit the school's dominant cultural and racial norms.

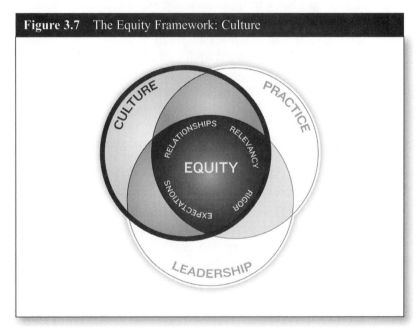

Figure 3.7   The Equity Framework: Culture

All educators and students can succeed when cultural understanding combines with the opportunity to learn, no matter how different they are from each other. As this equitable culture develops, the school starts thriving on its differences as an empowering force for growth and development.

According to Beverly Daniel Tatum, author of *Why Are All the Black Kids Sitting Together in the Cafeteria,* "When somebody feels alienated they're not likely learning. It's hard to intellectually engage if you're socially alienated. . . . When we create a climate of engagement, we want to think of both social and intellectual engagement" (as cited in VJE, 2006). The Equity Framework's culture strategies incorporate elements of racial awareness, professional attitudes, a clear focus on students, an inclusive environment, and collaboration among staff and the community:

- In building racial awareness, schools explicitly address race, and its impact upon the school. Race is the embodiment of difference. Our most fundamental assumptions and biases are tied directly to race, whether they are positive or negative. Diverse racial identities exist not only between races, but also within races. Without explicitly addressing race, educators limit their ability to understand the other diversities students bring with them tied to ethnicity, socioeconomics, gender, and language. By addressing race, racism, and institutionalized racism in the drive toward equity, educators directly challenge the traditional norms that have lead to only certain groups of primarily White students predictably succeeding and other groups such as Black male students predictably failing. Furthermore, once educators first learn how to address race in schools, they gain the necessary skills to deal with poverty and other issues that impact student learning.
- The professional attitudes of administrators and teachers dictate the school's ability to build equity. In particular, what are the true expectations that the school's educators hold for students? Furthermore, what is the responsibility that educators carry for their students' success? Without this culture of expectation and responsibility, teachers and administrators may blame students for low performance rather than claim ownership of student learning.
- By clearly focusing on students, teachers develop a broad understanding of the cultural backgrounds and learning characteristics of their students—and how these compare with their own cultural and learning traits. With this focus, schools also establish strong individualized learning goals for each student. While tied to the achievement of learning standards, these goals are tailored and supported according to the learning styles and needs of each student.

- To create an inclusive environment, schools must provide both safety and motivation that support *difference* within the educational institution. Safety provides not only physical security for students and teachers but also an environment where they can safely take risks in teaching and learning. Motivation corresponds directly with safety. Once teachers and students feel safe, motivation will push them to expand their skills and try harder to achieve. All students benefit from an inclusive environment, whether they are in special, general, or accelerated education programs.
- In successful schools, collaboration focuses not only on teacher teaming, but also on relationships with the community. By collaborating together from within and without, the school and its students can successfully build a school culture that guarantees equitable success for all students. Furthermore, empowering collaboration that involves multiple stakeholders creates a sustainable culture within the school of innovation and success.

THE EQUITY FRAMEWORK: PRACTICE

The practice strategies of the Equity Framework focus on what teachers do every day in the classroom, and how these things impact student achievement. According to educational consultant Jamie Almanzan, "If a kid fails in your class, you failed. We have got to start believing that teachers have something to do with it."

Pedagogy is the science and practice of teaching. It is the act of successfully educating our students. It is what a good teacher does every day. It can be practiced and studied. And, it can most definitely be improved. The Equity Framework strongly encourages the development of pedagogical *practice,* but not at the expense of improving *culture* and *leadership* within the school. When schools focus all of their professional development efforts just on pedagogical skills, it is akin to "drill and kill" teaching in the classroom since it is all about the things teachers do to students. Effective teaching practice occurs when good pedagogy happens in a context of strong culture and effective leadership.

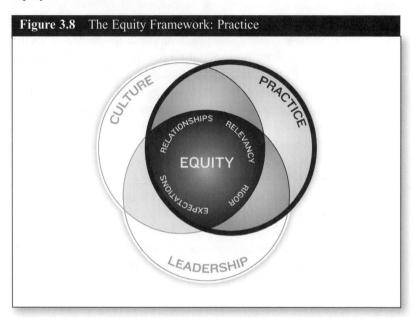

Figure 3.8   The Equity Framework: Practice

Within practice, the Equity Framework organizes effective classroom strategies inherent in good teaching, including curriculum, teaching skills, assessment, and interventions:

- An equitable curriculum is both standards driven and culturally relevant. Standards are designed to provide students with the skills and knowledge they need in order to succeed in society once they leave school. These standards, such as the nascent Common Core Standards in the United States, are most often measured through standardized exams. For students to succeed at these exams, the curriculum must be aligned with the standards that are tested. As described previously by the Northrich Elementary educators, this is not "teaching to the test," rather it is "teaching what is tested." For students to connect to these standards, however, the curriculum needs to be interesting and relevant to the student. Culturally relevant instruction is not simply about the heroes and holidays associated with the student's culture. Rather, it represents the current culture lived by the student, and all that represents in terms of neighborhood, heritage, family, history, and sociopolitical issues. Significant research by Gloria Ladson-Billings, Geneva Gay, Gail Thompson, Sonia Nieto, and others describes the impact of culturally relevant instruction. When standards are taught in a culturally relevant way, students are more likely to learn the curriculum.

- Strategies that develop equitable teaching skills build the educators' ability to support each student's individualized learning needs. Specifically, teachers acquire skills that improve their instructional delivery such as differentiation, effective strategies, and cooperative learning. Likewise, educators acquire learning strategies that help them engage and support all students.

- Strong assessment strategies maximize success in the classroom by allowing educators to know the reality of their teaching effectiveness. Assessment begins with the ability to collect and analyze both quantitative and qualitative data. Educators need to learn how to use this data in a formative way that not only assesses what students have learned but also guides what the teachers need to teach. As teachers understand more fully the power of assessment, they will learn how to modify and spiral their teaching in order to more equitably serve individual student learning needs.

- With an equitable curriculum, strong pedagogical skills, and effective assessment, educators will have what they need to create individualized interventions for struggling students. As every student receives the specific support they need, whether through tutoring and community mentoring programs or specialized attention and support in the school, achievement gaps will close and equity will grow.

The power of the Equity Framework is that it provides context and focuses a school's improvement efforts on equity for all students. It empowers teachers, coaches, administrators, and other school personnel to be true professional educators who can apply the necessary expertise in realizing the academic success of all students. The Equity Framework does not aim to dictate particular strategies or approaches. Rather, it connects the many different strategies and programs engaged by a school and school system in a focused and workable framework. As this happens, educators begin to understand how a particular leadership effort relates to the culture of the school and supports a developing teacher practice. The Equity Framework holistically organizes the strategies and efforts of a school and its educators so that true equity can be realized.

Equity Discussion

As a group, try to define the functioning framework that guides the programs and initiatives of your school and/or school system. In what ways can the Equity Framework serve to focus and direct your school improvement efforts?

Equity Lens: Professional

On the following equity lens chart, analyze the professional efforts that support you in the work you do in your classroom, school, and/or school system. This exercise asks you to identify in each section specific strategies you and/or your school currently use, plus strategies that you and/or your school could use to develop equitable *leadership, culture, and practice.* In each section, follow the prompts to identify equity-focused strategies that support and empower you as a professional educator. Reflect on this exercise with colleagues in your school and/or school system.

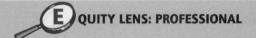

CULTURE

✓—List strategies you and/or your school currently use to create a safe and supportive learning environment:

?—List strategies you and/or your school could use to create a safe and supportive learning environment:

PRACTICE

✓—List strategies you and/or your school currently use to help you implement effective instructional practices:

?—List strategies you and/or your school could use to help you implement effective instructional practices:

EQUITY

LEADERSHIP

✓—List strategies you and/or your school currently use to empower you as a professional educator:

?—List strategies you and/or your school could use to empower you as a professional educator:

Using the Equity Framework, engage in an analysis of the primary improvement effort of your school or school system.

1. Describe the improvement effort, the professional development associated with it, and the strategies used to implement the effort in the classroom and/or school.

2. Determine if this improvement effort is primarily aimed at impacting leadership, culture, or practice.

3. Explain whether or not the improvement effort is balanced in its approach with the other two areas of the Equity Framework. For example, if the improvement effort impacts teacher practice, describe whether or not it is balanced and integrated with similar support to develop culture and leadership.

Share this analysis with a supervisor or colleague who directs the implementation of the improvement effort.

CHAPTER 4

Personal Equity

I once visited a classroom in rural Louisiana of a veteran teacher who had been very resistant to change. This school sat on the Mississippi River right in between two petrochemical plants. It was one of the poorest and lowest-achieving elementary schools in all of Louisiana. A colleague of mine, Steve Olsen, was contracted to work with this school over time. He was yet another in a long line of consultants paid to visit this school and help these teachers change how they taught students. I was surprised to hear that on Steve's first day in this school, he spent nearly half the day teaching a very simple formative assessment practice, fist-to-five. "Half the day!" I thought, "Wow, what about their belief systems? What about understanding their students better? What about leadership structures within the school?" These were typical things I believed needed to be addressed up front in a failing school. But, Steve spent half the day perfecting with these teachers a simple strategy that tells them whether or not their students have learned the lesson.

Then I heard from this veteran teacher about the impact this simple strategy had on her as an educator. She went back to her classroom the next day, taught her math lesson, and asked her students to show whether or not they understood the concept by holding up their hands in a fist if they did not understand at all, or up to five fingers if they fully understood the concept. When she asked them to show fist-to-five, her students held up nothing but fists and one finger.

Purely shocked that none of her students had learned what she just taught, she decided to teach the lesson once again, and again, and again over the next several days until every student in her class was holding up four and five fingers.

Never in her entire career had she realized that her students' lack of learning had something to do with her rather than with them. A few weeks later, when Steve was back at the school for the second day of training, this formerly resistant veteran teacher marched right up to him and pleasantly demanded, "What else do you have for me?" In all of her many years of teaching, she had never known that the reason her students failed was because of her own ineffective teaching rather than her students perceived lack of interest in learning. She now knew that she held the responsibility in her classroom for student learning, and has been a different teacher ever since.

Most educators deserve to feel proud for an individual job well done. But a school or school system is really only as good as its least effective educator. My high school football coach often said that the team was only as good as its weakest player. We once lost because of me—I was that weakest player who had too many fumbles, and too many missed blocks. Despite a strong team effort, we once lost in the playoffs because of critical mistakes made by a couple of players. I can blame that senior year playoff loss on my teammates, but in the end, it is the team that wins or loses based on how the various individuals perform.

Schools and school systems are the same—they are only as strong as the weakest teacher or administrator on staff, despite the dedicated and heroic efforts of their best educators. In order to succeed through the end of high school, a student needs to spend the majority of his or her school years with effective teachers, as a year here or there with a great teacher cannot make up for the lack of a student's learning in one or two years with an ineffective teacher. This is why the search for systemic educational equity begins within each of us personally. Unless every one of us commits ourselves to pursuing equity for each and every student, no institution can overcome our individual deficiencies.

In all the schools I have observed that have closed and eliminated their achievement gaps, the educators have always been remarkably authentic. Their efforts to build equity were not for their own recognition, or because some outside entity had "forced" them to do this. Some schools and educators may have started the process because of a disciplinary action, but this is not why they ultimately succeeded at equitizing their school. They built equity because they developed a great sense of responsibility for the learning of all their students. These educators did not wait for the legislature to fund their schools, or for the students' parents to show up and help out. They were driven by the powerful realization that each of them personally has significant impact upon the academic success (or failure) of their students—equitable educators see no valid excuse for not succeeding with every student.

Centering yourself in equity begins with a personal acknowledgment of who you are as a person and what constitutes your own belief systems, then authenticating those beliefs in your actions, and finally claiming full responsibility as a professional educator—an exciting "journey to racial literacy" as described by Bonnie Davis (2009). As you center yourself within equity, you will find the strength, conviction, courage, and voice necessary to be an active participant in building institutional equity, the subject of the next chapter. But without *your* personal engagement as an equitable educator, can your school or school system ever be fully equitable?

EQUITY SUCCESS: FRANKFORD ELEMENTARY

Powerful examples of educational equity are often found in unexpected places. Driving up to Frankford Elementary in Frankford, Delaware, I noticed the farms surrounding the school. It was a long drive from nearly anywhere. But the U.S. assistant secretary of education had just visited this rural school to recognize its remarkable turnaround in student achievement. We were looking forward to documenting how Frankford went from one of the lowest-performing elementary schools in Delaware to the annual number-one or number-two school in the state.

According to Sharon Brittingham, the principal,

When I first came here, when I was first hired, there was a mandate from the superintendent that things had to change at Frankford. I did not want to know where the students lived. I did not want to know who their parents were. I did not want to know what their IQ was. I just wanted to know that you the teacher could have growth with the child. I think in the beginning, teachers did not have the belief in themselves that they could make it work for all kids.

Frankford Elementary sits in a poor rural chicken-farming area of Delaware. The school is evenly divided between White, Black, and Latino students; 76 percent of the students are on free and reduced-price lunch, 22 percent of students are designated for special education, and 23 percent of students are English language learners. Demographically, this is a school that was historically excused for lower student achievement, but that dramatically changed under the leadership of Sharon Brittingham, a veteran White principal who—though soft-spoken—was firmly in charge.

Fourth-grade teacher Kimberlee Kleinstuber describes that when she first came to the school, she had a certain expectation of what she was going to experience in her classroom based on the student profiles. Sharon shares that the teachers "believed that all kids could learn, but most kids could only learn a certain amount." At Frankford, failure with students was no longer an option.

Tracy Hudson, reading specialist at Frankford, recalls the beginning of her teaching career: "It could be a lonely profession—you get in your classroom; you're there by yourself." Teaming and collaboration became one of the first objectives that Sharon implemented in the school. Yet, she struggled to convince the staff that teaming worked. So, she recruited a teacher to the school with whom she had previously worked who knew how to effectively collaborate. This provided another teacher on staff who could model and build trust in the collaborative process. Fifth-grade teacher David Grise shares that "it's a hard thing when you start these professional learning communities. You don't want to be the person who sits there and says, 'My kids are struggling.'"

The school recognized that they needed to honor the individual learning needs of every student. According to Sharon, "It's as though we created an IEP [Individual Education Plan] for every student." Rather than just students in special education receiving individual focus and planning, every student at Frankford—the high, low, and average performers—were supported daily in their personal learning needs, leading them toward clearly set learning targets.

Once the capacity of the teachers started growing as a result of their PLCs, the staff realized that there was nothing they could not do—and would not do—to create a successful environment for their students. The simple question of "what's good for the kids?" became the driver of what the school did for its students in creating numerous strong approaches to increase student achievement.

One of these ideas is a highly successful mentoring program wherein the school gets well over one hundred parents and community members who sit down and work one-on-one with individual students each week. This is a school that cannot rely upon highly educated parents or a nearby college or university for its mentors. But they realized that any community member—no matter their education—can spend valuable time with a student each week. An immigrant Latino parent with only a fifth-grade education is still capable of sitting down and reading with a first-grade English language learning student. Innovative ideas like this brought great benefit to Frankford—and at zero increase to the budget since the mentoring is all volunteer.

Reading specialist Jennifer Babcock states that teachers now "take ownership. They don't come to me and say, 'I've got this student—you take care of him.' They come and they say, 'I have a problem. What can I do to help [the student]?'" The culture of the school is such that teachers can try innovative practices and if something doesn't work, they feel safe to admit it and get additional assistance to succeed at the new teaching methodology. Jennifer continues, explaining that teachers "are not admitting defeat. They are just trying to find what's best for the student in their classroom."

Data played a huge role in the culture change of the school. Sharon says, "[The] data is not lying about what is happening—that these children are being successful." Remarkably, student achievement at Frankford Elementary is now at the following level:

- Since 2003, over 90 percent of all students have met state standard in every subject area.
- For several years in a row, 100 percent of students met state standard in reading and science.

Tracy shares further how these new strategies influenced her role as one of the reading specialists: "When teachers saw that they were being successful, they wanted the change. They wanted to do the things that we were talking about."

One of the strongest moments of impact on the school, according to Sharon, occurred "when we had students that were in our intensive learning center, the lowest-functioning students, pass the state test—I think that was a big turning point." Seeing the success and growth in their own school has a profound impact upon the expectations and drive of the staff toward higher achievement.

As illustrated in the equity lens for Frankford Elementary that follows, a combination of appropriate student learning strategies with a belief system focused on the learning of the students led to equity for all students.

Frankford Elementary has received numerous honors since achieving this success, including Education Trust's Dispelling the Myth Award. In a diverse school with no racial, gender, or economic achievement inequities, success is a given for all students. According to Kimberlee, "I think we found the formula. The formula is not one teacher here, and one teacher there, it's the package."

Figure 4.1   Equity Lens: Frankford Elementary

CULTURE

Personal Strategies

- Change culture toward high expectations for all.
- Courageously evaluate and share educators' weaknesses.

Institutional Strategies

- Incorporate PLCs for all teachers to build collaboration.
- Outreach to community resulting in over one hundred mentors.

Professional Strategies

- Create individual education plans (IEPs) for every student— whether a high, low, or average performer.
- Empower teachers to understand individual student learning needs.

PRACTICE

Personal Strategies

- Expect teachers to master instructional strategies.
- Fine-tune daily practice and problem solving in instruction.

Institutional Strategies

- Provide professional development that models strategies across the school.
- Implement rigorous standards-based instruction.

Professional Strategies

- Implement individual student learning plans with fidelity.
- Share effective pedagogical practices in teams and across grade levels.

EQUITY

LEADERSHIP

Personal Strategies

- Challenge teachers to change their level of expectations for students.
- Facilitate procedures for teachers to no longer be isolated in their practice.

Institutional Strategies

- Clearly communicate learning goals to faculty, students, and the community.
- Disseminate knowledge of school improvement strategies among staff.

Professional Strategies

- Provide professional development that disseminates best practices of teachers within the school.
- Provide support to all teachers in improving their practice.

Individual Collectivism

As illustrated at Frankford Elementary, the search for equity begins within each of us personally. For me to be equitable means that I must recognize honestly where I come from, my own biases and beliefs, and the lens through which I look upon the world. Rosemary Henze and colleagues, in *Leading for Diversity,* write:

> It is a recipe for conflict to act in the world based on the assumption that we have an objective view of it. In contrast, to assume that we each have a valid view of the world and have something to learn from each other's perspectives is the basis for mutual respect and appreciation. (Henze, Katz, Norte, Sather, & Walker, 2002, p. 20)

The essence of equity is that each of us must develop the necessary skills to treat the collective of diverse people around us with the same degree of hope, aspiration, and positive expectation that we afford ourselves.

As I center myself in equity, I become aware of how my race, culture, and background impact the way I see and interpret others. Growing up privileged within society, White middle-class people do not always intuitively offer others who differ from the norm the same amount of respect and dignity they afford themselves. The basis of White privilege in Western society is the assumption that one's own way of thinking and living is inherently the *right* way. To be in a position of privilege and surrounded by people like myself, it feels natural to assume that the whole world is just like me. But equity is not about just creating equality or trying to make others fit our perceived norms; it is about individualizing fairness, justice, and opportunity for everyone, regardless of whether or not they fit the dominant norm.

This tension between the "norm" and diversity in U.S. society stems from the very origin of this country. From the beginning, we have been challenged to describe ourselves either as a nation of individuals or as a nation with a collective identity. In describing the tension between the individual and the collective in U.S. society, Carlos Cortes (2002) describes the delicate balancing act found within the U.S. Constitution's emphasis on *pluribus unum:*

Such *pluribus* values as freedom, individualism, and diversity live in constant and inevitable tension with such *unum* values as authority, conformity, and commonality . . . because the United States began and has evolved not just as a nation of individuals, but also as a nation of groups—racial, ethnic, religious, and cultural groups, to name just a few. (p. 145)

I have often observed individuals espousing a *pluribus* belief that emphasizes the individual, but acting in a *unum* approach wherein another's diverse individuality threatens the collective security of one's affinity groups. This likely leads to the subconscious thought, "If they were only more like me, this might not be a problem." But equity demands that we recognize the individual while valuing the collective—it is the act of consciously honoring both perspectives.

OVERCOMING BIASES

This need to equitably honor *pluribus unum* begins with overcoming one's biases and stereotypes. This is harder than it may appear. Just because we may care for someone different from ourselves does not necessarily mean we have overcome prejudice toward that individual or people like that person. In the book *Freedom Writers Diary,* teacher Erin Gruwell (1999) writes about facing stiff opposition from other teachers who did not believe it was appropriate to treat her unruly and disengaged students as high-level learners. Their opposition wasn't from a lack of caring, as the other teachers were also dedicated educators. Rather, these teachers allowed their biases and prejudices to influence their teaching in a way that placed these students at a disadvantage.

Internal biases such as these lead to lowered expectations, especially for students who differ from the norm. If a teacher does not internally believe that a student is capable of learning at a high level, it is very unlikely the teacher will instruct the student to that level. Several times, I have met educators of Color who speak of going to the parent-teacher conferences for their own children, and having to convince the teacher that their child is capable of the highest levels of learning. The most effective educators, however, overcome their own internal biases and lowered expectations for disadvantaged students. Students succeed in these classrooms because they know the teacher individually believes in them. These successful teachers move past the idea that treating all students the same reflects their caring and fairness—they recognize the inequities of equal treatment

Similarly, the belief in color-blindness continues to be one of the most destructive and inequitable mind-sets in today's schools. Even though it is purported to be an "open-minded" way of thinking, it can severely restrict a person of Color's chances for success in a diverse world. This is because it allows those of us in the majority to ignore the foremost identifier of diversity—one's race. As discussed earlier, color-blindness is especially pernicious because we actually *see* race—outside of physical blindness, it is impossible not to see the skin color of another.

Eduardo Bonilla-Silva (2006) describes color-blindness as "racism without racists" (p. 1). A person who claims color-blindness permits him- or herself to maintain subconscious biases and prejudice, but under the guise of acceptance. It is tolerance of difference without validation of equal worth. Bonilla-Silva goes on to describe the benefits of this approach for White people, specifically, "The beauty of this new ideology is that it aids in the maintenance of White privilege without fanfare, without naming those who it subjects and those who it rewards" (p. 3).

Race is real. Even though the labels and values associated with racial identity are historical social and political constructions designed to differentiate between communities and justify prejudiced treatment, the identity of skin color—race—is ever present. Thus, race may technically be a label that identifies one's skin pigmentation, but the judgments, privileges, and oppression based on this perception of race persist. According to straightforward racial identifiers that avoid ethnicity, I am White, my friends and colleagues are Black, Brown, Yellow, and Red. In identifying my own race and the race of others, I acknowledge not only our ancestral heritages, but also our differing present-day realities. Color-blindness attempts to erase the stunning diversity around us, thus forcing each of us into an indistinguishable norm.

Overcoming our personal and internal biases, stereotypes, and prejudices begins with an honest acknowledgment that they actually exist within us. Rosemary Henze and coauthors (2002), in *Leading for Diversity,* state:

> As educators, it is especially important for us to recognize that
> we, too, are subjective and that this is a part of being human. We
> don't need to feel guilty about being subjective and, in fact,
> coming to terms with our subjectivity frees us to move around
> the circle of perception. (pp. 20–21)

With this increased consciousness comes the ability to check our
assumptions at the door and accept and treat others as they really are
without forcing them into our preformed prejudices.

Stereotypes develop over time because of generalized traits that
stand in contrast to dominant norms. Our society is dominated by
White cultural values. White people as well as people of Color are
constantly subjected to these values, and thus we all easily connect
with associated stereotypes. One stereotype of African Americans is
that they are loud and physical. This stands in contrast to the traditional White value of being reserved and soft-spoken. Of course, not
all Black people are loud and physical, just as not all White people
are reserved and soft-spoken. But, White people encounter few negative judgments based upon being quiet and unassuming, whereas
there are significant negative judgments Black people hear because
they stand in contrast to the traditional White norm.

As a White person working toward equity, I especially must
acknowledge my own limitations toward diversity, which come from
growing up heavily exposed to stereotypes of all sorts. This begins
with understanding my own Whiteness as a precursor to understanding the differences in others. In *How to Teach Students Who Don't
Look Like You,* Bonnie Davis (2006) writes:

> If I, as a White educator, do not understand what Whiteness
> brings to my diverse classroom, I lack important information.
> What does it mean to be White in America? . . . If I am White,
> I don't have to think about it unless I choose to put myself into
> a minority position or am forced into one. Yet people of Color
> do not have that option. (p. 55)

ACKNOWLEDGING PRIVILEGE

After engaging in honest self-reflection, the privileges associated
with being White become readily apparent. I have never been the

victim of racial profiling from law enforcement. This means that when I am pulled over while driving, I have been caught breaking the law. Not until after personally hearing the stories of numerous persons of Color being victimized by racial profiling did I finally believe it was happening. Being victimized because of my race has never been part of my reality and, hence, it is easy to let this aspect of White privilege remain hidden from my view.

The challenge with racial privilege is that the recipient does not need to know of its existence in order to benefit from it. Thus, an assumption grows within the recipient that the privileges granted unto him or her is just the way the world operates. If I am never profiled racially while driving, there is no necessity for me to understand racial profiling. When my privilege compels me to believe that my paradigm is the only truth, it is easy to dismiss contrasting paradigms when presented by those who differ from myself.

White people, perhaps unknowingly, tend to assign blame rather than empathy when hearing of racial inequities. This stems from a conflicting view of difference between White culture and people of Color. For someone who is White, difference often feels like a choice rather than a reality. Whites typically work to either hide their differences and "blend in," or highlight their differences in order to prove their individualism. People of Color cannot hide their racial difference—it is an unalterable reality. Hence, Whites tend to project choice of difference upon people of Color. This especially manifests itself in schools. Students who struggle are most often blamed for *choosing* not to work hard, *choosing* not to care, and ultimately *choosing* not to succeed. But, the student of Color understands that his or her difference from the school's dominant norm is a reality and not a choice—it is the student's reality that the educators do not understand the student, where the student comes from, nor how the student learns. Thus, when addressing inequities, educators must begin by choosing to meet the student at his or her reality in order to help them succeed in school.

At the same time, unacknowledged privilege limits an educator's ability to address racialized inequities. Consider the following thoughts about White privilege by Peggy McIntosh (1989), a professor at Wellesley College:

I think Whites are carefully taught not to recognize White privilege, as males are taught not to recognize male privilege.

So I have begun in an untutored way to ask what it is like to
have White privilege. I have come to see White privilege as an
invisible package of unearned assets that I can count on cashing
in each day, but about which I was "meant" to remain oblivious.
White privilege is like an invisible weightless knapsack of special provisions, maps, passports, codebooks, visas, clothes, tools,
and blank checks. (p. 10)

Adding up my privileges because of my Whiteness, I realize that
I have never been accused of shoplifting, never been frisked, and
never been suspected of laziness, anger, or a lack of intelligence or
talent just because of my race. Even more powerful, I have often
benefitted from other's assumptions in me of intelligence, capabilities, and likelihood to succeed just because of my color. After recognizing my White privilege, I am deeply compelled to ask whether
my son Dominic and my daughter Maya will experience the same
privileges I have enjoyed, or will they face prejudices that I have
never personally experienced? Likewise, can today's students benefit from an assumption of success like I did? Or, if I am a White
teacher, do my unacknowledged privileges actually prevent my students of Color from receiving the education they need simply
because I am thrusting my privileged paradigms upon them and not
instructing them within their own reality?

MISSIONARY SYNDROME

In his book *We Can't Teach What We Don't Know,* multicultural
author Gary Howard (1999) describes his time as a student at Yale
when, as a White person, he moved to "the Hill" of New Haven,
Connecticut, a primarily Black inner-city enclave, to work with poor
Black and Hispanic youth at the YMCA. He lived on the Hill during
the civil rights riots of 1968 when blocks all around him burned to
the ground. This was a pinnacle moment for Howard as he discovered that the anxiety and despair felt by the ethnic communities
surrounding him were real, and that a young White guy from the
suburbs couldn't exactly bring them hope just because of his good
intentions.

He describes this time as his "missionary" phase—he was the
enlightened individual coming with the "answers" to show the

destitute a better way to live. Reflecting on this period, Howard (1999) writes, "How can White Americans, those who have never been touched viscerally by the realities of race, break out of their cultural isolation and ignorance?" Howard continues, "I didn't realize it at the time, but this naïve missionary period was merely the tentative beginning of a long journey toward multicultural awareness" (p. 14).

The *missionary syndrome* is a condescending attitude that good-meaning people carry when trying to help others "less fortunate" than themselves. It is purely tied to privilege—when we have much and society works for us, then it appears easy to help others because if they were just "more like me" (a subconscious thought), they might overcome their challenges. By no means should we avoid helping others, for the very purpose of education is giving people the tools they need to succeed in life and in society. It is the approach that matters.

Authenticity within us as exhibited in our motives and attitudes is critical to accomplishing equity at the personal level. Authenticity is realness in purpose, honesty in beliefs and understandings, and integrity in our relations with others. Authenticity also helps us value a situation for both its potential and limitations. Educators are often either optimistic or pessimistic about what a school can accomplish. When centering one's self in equity, we need both. A simple formula follows:

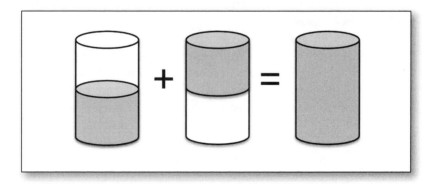

A cup half-full (optimism) +
a cup half-empty (pessimism) = a full cup

To accomplish equity within a school requires that the educators look both at what they are good at, and where they struggle—the full cup of education. So many answers already exist within schools—some struggling students succeed with one teacher but not with others—but schools often lack the culture and tools to authentically assess why some teachers find success and others do not.

Without authenticity about who we are and why we do what we do, we cannot center ourselves in equity because we have not fully valued the diversity surrounding us. Without authenticity in our work as educators, we can never fully achieve equity because this allows us to continuously measure our students by how much they differ from us and the norm, rather than seeing them as equal to ourselves in hope, aspiration, and potential—and worthy of our very best efforts.

PERSONAL EQUITY EQUALS PASSION

Bonnie Davis (2009) writes, "When we approach others with our authentic selves and our body language is congruent with our words, we tend to win them over. Then we connect as human beings who respect each other as unique individuals" (p. 33). In *personal equity,* we must ask whether we have authentic passion for the daily work of changing schools and increasing student performance. Passion is both an enabling and sustaining force in equitizing education—it allows us to take on the tough challenges of persistent achievement inequities and stick with this work even when obstacles and resistance confront us head-on. The key characteristic of our personal equity work is *passion.*

Equity work can most challenge educators when it becomes evident that their "tried and true" practices are simply not serving their diverse students. Every teacher and administrator working today—regardless of race—figured out how to succeed in the system at some point. When most educators were students, the status quo served them well. Thus, educators often conclude that what worked for them should serve today's students equally well. This is when one's own successful background becomes an obstacle to accomplishing equity. Raymond Terrell and Randall Lindsey (2009) write that "reaction to equity issues is often dependent on one's own experiences as a student" (p. 11). An equitable educator will acknowledge that *just because it worked for me does not mean it works for my students.* Passion for equity leads to a creative process of building a new educational system that works for *all* students and *all* educators *all* of the time.

To sustain this passion requires acknowledging the barriers that can neutralize passionate dedication to equity, both individually and collectively. In the *Moral Imperative of School Leadership,* Michael Fullan (2003) lists five self-imposed barriers to school change that prevent individual educational leaders from acting proactively (commentary added in italics):

1. Perceived system limitations *(out of my control).*

2. If-only dependency *(if only x would happen, then I could . . .).*

3. Loss of moral compass *(becoming overloaded with tasks rather than purpose).*

4. Inability to take charge of one's own learning *(just tell me how to . . .).*

5. Responsibility virus *(overresponsibility and underresponsibility).* (p. 17)

By addressing these obstacles forthright, we gain the strength to overcome them and progress toward equity. Personal equity always reverts back to honestly assessing who we are and why we do what we do. It is on-all-the-time consciousness that allows us to quickly assess, change our actions, and empathetically respond to others as we equitize our practice.

According to Gary Howard (1999),

We cannot fully and fruitfully engage in meaningful dialogue across the differences of race and culture without doing the work of personal transformation. If we as White educators are not deeply moved and transformed, there is little hope that anything else will significantly shift. . . . We cannot help our students overcome the negative repercussions of past and present racial dominance if we have not unraveled the remnants of dominance that still lingers in our minds, hearts, and habits. (p. 4)

EQUITY IN ACTION: CHAPTER 4, PERSONAL EQUITY

Equity Discussion

Discuss with a colleague your understanding of equity, especially as it relates to your own privilege and difference. What experiences do you draw upon to help others succeed, such as students and educators? In what ways do these experiences resonate with your discussion partner? Can the person relate, or are your experiences disconnected from your partner's reality?

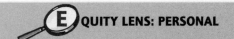

EQUITY LENS: PERSONAL

My colleague and friend Jamie Almanzan has often said, "We teach first who we are," which means that when we teach or work in a school, our own ethnicity, race, culture, and background comes out first in our actions and efforts with students and colleagues alike. Apply the equity lens to your own understanding of personal equity by engaging in the following reflections:

Who Are You?

Identify your race, socioeconomic status, ethnicity, gender, culture, sexual orientation, and politics. In what ways do these traits impact how you describe yourself as an educator? How are these traits similar or different from the students in your classroom, school, and/or school system?

What Do You Believe?

Based on the characteristics you identified in the previous section, what values do you hold and what matters to you in regards to education? How is this similar or different from the students in your classroom, school, and/or school system?

What Do You Do?

Related to the characteristics you identified in the previous sections, describe what you do or don't do as an educator to build equity for each and every one of your students. How do your actions serve or not serve the individual students in your classroom, school, and/ or school system?

EQUITY ACTION #4

Identify what you need to do personally to center yourself in equity so as to ensure that *all* students under your supervision receive an equitable education. Describe your commitment to equity both in terms of your internal work around your own beliefs, understandings, and expectations, and your external actions toward your students and colleagues. Engage in changing one of these things you identified.

Deepening Equity: Personal Reflection

Whether White or of Color, analyze yourself according to the characteristics of Whiteness. What privileges, beliefs, and/or expectations do you have related to the norms and experiences of majority culture? How does this impact your ability to address biases and challenge stereotypes, both in your personal life and your work as an educator?

CHAPTER 5

Institutional Equity

Recently, I worked in Jones County, Georgia. At lunch, Verneda Appling, a kind and quiet African American woman who was only days away from retiring as assistant superintendent, engaged me in conversation about the morning's training. With the district leadership, we had engaged in a great discussion defining equity and describing what it looks like. Putting forth one additional effort to positively impact the school system she had so faithfully served, Appling leaned over toward me and said, "It's only equity if they actually do it."

To reiterate, the definition of *equity* works to describe what an equitable classroom, school, and school system looks like:

Educators provide all students with the individual support they need to reach and exceed a common standard.

A viable challenge to this definition is to ask, so what? Once equity is defined, what does one do with it? Operationalizing equity requires educators to formally change the way things operate in order to equitize the system—the institution itself must change. Working with Verneda, we created a definition for *institutionalized equity:*

Institutionalized policies, processes, and practices that guarantee educators provide all students with the individual support they need to reach and exceed a common standard or expectation.

Institutionalized equity guarantees students receive the individualized support they need to succeed in school because the school and school system—the institution—formally integrates equity into its day-to-day, year-to-year operations.

As stated previously, a school or school system is only as good as its weakest educators. Despite belief statements and proclamations, without actually changing the culture, practices, and structures of the school or school system to support equity, inequity remains. Dennis Littky, founder and director of the successful "Met" School in Providence, Rhode Island, succinctly states, "If we care about kids more than we care about schools, then we must change schools" (Littky & Grabelle, 2004, p. 28).

Equity requires change. Equity is foundational in any school or system that hopes to lift all students to high levels of achievement. Schools and school systems, however, are conservative institutions in that they do not change quickly. Even though they may be populated with well-meaning forward-thinking individuals, the educational institutions themselves tend to perpetuate the status quo. This is *institutionalism*—when an organization works primarily to maintain and protect status and tradition. Education has a long history of institutionalism as evidenced by the following:

- The inability of public education to rapidly adjust to students' needs.
- The perpetual dropout of so many students, especially those of Color.
- The unreversed racial achievement inequities, despite much public effort.
- The collective resistance of U.S. educators against the original goal of No Child Left Behind: all students at grade level by 2014.
- The time and effort spent by educational leaders on adult issues rather than student learning: tenure, labor, politics, community issues, and parental demands unrelated to the needs of struggling students.
- Pride in tradition and pats on the back for a "job well done," despite student failures.

All of these things point to a school or school system's desire to serve itself, to protect its honor and dignity, and serve first the needs of the adults at the expense of true equitable change for students.

When the institution puts kids first, however, real change can happen that leads to equity for all.

EQUITY SUCCESS:
SANGER UNIFIED SCHOOL DISTRICT

My wife grew up in the town of Sanger, California, a small farming community in California's Central Valley. Knowing this town well, I was surprised to learn that Sanger Unified School District was one of the most successful turnaround districts in the state. My previous perceptions of Sanger schools were that there was strong support of football, but little emphasis on academic success. With 80 percent of its students Latino and Hmong, sky-high poverty rates, a large English language learning (ELL) population, and few college-educated parents, Sanger schools had never been expected to do much. But I knew remarkable things were happening when I heard that three of the thirty-five California Blue Ribbon Schools in 2009 were in Sanger—a system of only nineteen schools.

Superintendent Marc Johnson describes the district as focused on the needs of adults rather than children when he arrived in 1999 as an assistant superintendent. "We really had turmoil in terms of fractured relations, broken trust, and dysfunctional communication. When our superintendent left, our board felt that this district had been a meat grinder in terms of leadership stability."

Marc has the presence of a football coach—strong and obvious leadership, but also deep caring and love for the educators and students in Sanger. He and most of the district leadership are White and middle class in a community that is primarily Latino and agricultural. Several years earlier, Sanger Unified received a letter from the California Department of Education stating that the system was a "program improvement district"—a sanctioning that could allow the state to take over and entirely restructure. As Marc describes,

> We really needed a wake-up call to bring us to the point that we recognized that our job was to do a really good job with all kids. That is what happened to us when we got that letter from Sacramento. . . . We met two days after we got that letter with our whole administrative team and we laid out what this meant. It was a very tense time. . . . At the end of

the conversation, I asked, "Does anyone have a question, anything you want to say?" One of the principals spoke up and said, "You know Marc, you have always told us that we don't have problems, we have opportunities. And, as far as I'm concerned, this label is not a problem, it is an opportunity for us to begin to do the work that to this day we have not been doing."

Rather than pointing fingers, Sanger Unified established lines of communication, built trust, and focused on reshaping their institutional culture. Data became the base for open and honest communication about student learning. According to Marc, "That became the framework. Having data is wonderful, but it is meaningless unless you also respond to the data." Through a combination of professional learning communities (PLCs), intensive daily response to intervention (RTI), and focused analysis based on classroom data, Sanger Unified embarked on a remarkable seven-year journey to success.

Five years ago at Sanger Unified's John S. Wash Elementary, only about 35 percent of the sixth graders were proficient or advanced. In 2009, the educators of Wash Elementary had lifted over 90 percent of the sixth graders to proficient or advanced levels, leading to its designation as a 2009 Blue Ribbon School for its dramatic increase in student achievement. A school motto announces "Every child, every day, whatever it takes!" According to the principal, Wes Seever, "If you have a good consistent program, more and more kids will graduate from your program proficient and advanced."

Change at Wash Elementary, however, was not instant. When the school's student body went from 20 percent to over 50 percent English language learners, teachers had to conclude, "I can't teach the same way." Previously, the culture of the school had never pushed the teachers to focus on specific student learning needs.

As described by Wes, "With some of these programs, like PLCs, I wasn't sure about them; I didn't know what they looked like. But all I knew was that I had to do them, because if I was not doing them, it was very clear that I was not doing my job." Wes is an enthusiastic principal—easy to trust and passionate about the work. The first thing he did was sit down with each teacher, explain the purpose of the changes, and explore their concerns. "I came to believe that this is what we are supposed to do," he explains. "I had to go into teacher's classrooms, because just me saying 'we have to do this' doesn't change their beliefs or attitudes. But what changes their beliefs or attitudes is when they try it."

As the staff focused on implementing new instructional practices in the classroom, collaborating, and studying weekly data related to their efforts, teachers got on board as they now clearly saw the results of their teaching. The data illustrated the failure of the teachers in their teaching, rather than the failure of the students in their learning. As the school changed, so did the teachers, and thus the achievement of the students. "These practices we have in place right now—the teachers believe in them. They know that it is important to collaborate as a team." When this happens, the students become the deserving beneficiaries.

"We were very clear on the things that all schools will do," describes Marc Johnson. "[Schools] will provide interventions. They will provide supports for English language learners. Those things are nonnegotiable." Early on, the district quickly acknowledged every success and publicized it widely. By doing this, belief in the collective capacity of the district to serve all students grew dramatically—*if others can do it, why can't we?* Marc describes the transformation: "As we saw our students become successful—that is the bottom line, growth in student achievement—we began to see a deeper belief on the part of the adults in the children."

Arriving at Washington Academic Middle School (WAMS) in Sanger, the principal, John Yost, says he found "a lot of great people, a lot of random acts of improvement, a lot of good things happening, but no systems in place." With 40 percent of the WAMS students designated as English language learners, these "random acts of improvement" were not institutionalized in a school that John describes as "kind of going through the motions."

Over the next few years, WAMS changed its culture from focusing on the teaching of the educator to the learning of the student. To move the school toward greater collective capacity, they learned how to understand and use data—a practice that had never been part of the culture. As described by John,

It was a great starting point because teachers were looking at data and examining whether we are teaching, or are we just presenting—are kids learning? And so that really allowed us as a team to have that common language, that common voice, that common dialogue. Before we had nothing to anchor on to.

As WAMS studied successful schools and changed its culture and practices, synergy grew among the staff as a whole. WAMS teachers found greater satisfaction in their work as they discovered that they were capable of succeeding with all their students. Individual teachers realized they had the power to not only change their own classrooms, but also those of their colleagues, and ultimately the school as a whole.

"It's the actions of the adults that make the difference. Kids are kids, and one of our core beliefs is that we never blame the kids," states John. "These kids can learn at high levels just like anyone else. So, if we want them to learn at high levels, we have to examine what are we doing that influences learning."

The development of a collaborative culture allowed Sanger Unified to support the implementation of multiple improvement efforts, including a highly effective RTI program. Sanger's RTI efforts guide teachers in continuously supporting students until they master the content through three tiers or levels of instruction: the whole classroom, pull-out support groups, and individualized interventions. According to Marc Johnson, "Historically, teachers would finish a chapter, give a test, look at the results and say, 'Oh my gosh, 30 percent of my kids failed this, but I've got to finish the book.'" Through RTI, rigorous awareness of each student's progress allows teacher teams to focus instruction individually so that each student finds academic success.

Sanger Unified School District also engages in *collaborative competition* among the schools. As described by Michael Fullan (2010), collaborative competition is when schools work together to improve collective capacity, but drive each other's success higher and higher as they try to outperform one another. In Sanger, PLCs are formed between schools at the principal and teacher level. Monthly, these interschool PLCs share and analyze data together. According to Wash Elementary's principal, Wes Seever,

We get data by grade level and by school for every school in the district, so if my third grade is not performing, I can look at all of the performance data from all of the third grades in the district. My third grade [teachers] went to another school in the district because their third grade was outperforming our school. And we wanted to know, what are they doing that we are not? If they can do it, why can't we?

Marc Johnson describes, "Our district was very competitive, but we also played our cards very close to the chest. Today, that competition is still, 'my goal is to outperform you, but you and I will both improve.'" Prior to these efforts, teachers habitually worked in isolation, unaware of what the data might say about their teaching, and how to improve it. Now, teachers collaborate daily with school colleagues, monthly with district colleagues, and experience the success that comes with institutionalizing equity and success for adults and students alike.

As illustrated in the equity lens for Sanger Unified School District that follows, the district has built systemic and institutionalized equity. Sanger did not do this just by focusing on one area of improvement. Rather, they institutionally changed leadership, culture, and practice in order to accelerate and perpetuate systemic improvement.

Almost no other district in California has increased student achievement at a more rapid pace. Over the last seven years, Sanger Unified School District has doubled overall student achievement. They have dramatically changed the culture of the institution—the norms of the school system now focus entirely upon the students, and not the adults. It is truly a system worthy of all its accolades, and living proof that systemwide equity reform can be achieved.

Figure 5.1   Equity Lens: Sanger Unified School District

CULTURE

Personal Strategies

- Examine what failure meant for the students.
- Strongly support personal capacity building of teachers.

Institutional Strategies

- Implement PLCs at every school and every team.
- Implement culturally responsive programs, such as those for ELLs.

Professional Strategies

- Schedule and support teacher collaboration.
- Empower teachers to understand individual student learning needs.

PRACTICE

Personal Strategies

- Support teachers in effectively instructing all students daily.
- Expect teachers to master instructional strategies.

Institutional Strategies

- Implement RTI with Tier 3 instruction in every school.
- Implement rigorous standards-based instruction.

Professional Strategies

- Intensely and regularly analyze student data based on team-developed assessments.
- Share effective pedagogical practices in teams, across grade levels, and between schools.

EQUITY

LEADERSHIP

Personal Strategies

- Take personal responsibility for achievement—for administrators and teachers alike.
- Support administrators and teachers if they engage in change effort, and hold accountable if resistant.

Institutional Strategies

- Establish interschool collaboration and competition.
- Establish districtwide goals and focus.

Professional Strategies

- Focus professional development on formative assessment to allow educators to effectively use data.
- Institutionalize systemic programs like PLCs and RTI in every school.

UNDERSTANDING INSTITUTIONALISM

The challenge with institutionalism is that educational institutions outlive individuals. Change is a challenge because the institution itself is the constant. All members of the institution collectively represent the values and attributes of the institution, whether or not the individual personally agrees. In other words, the institution is far more powerful than the individual. Consequently, to change a school or school system requires as much focus on changing the whole institution as it does on changing the individuals within the institution.

Institutionalism happens when a dominant power or force systematizes an organization to serve its own values. As stated by Lindsey, Nuri Robins, and Terrell (2003) in *Cultural Proficiency,*

> The dominant culture has disproportionately greater political and economic power in a society. . . . Each person in the school is represented by several types of cultures. It is from this amalgam of culture types that the dominant cultural patterns emerge within the school. As the school culture's dominant pattern emerges, it either embraces or marginalizes educators, parents, and students of dominated cultural groups. (p. 42)

What those in power see as preferable or good is institutionalized as the norm for everyone else. Typically what is lost is value and respect toward those who differ from the norm.

For example, the historical canon of great literature has always been White- and Western European-centric. The reasons why this happened are rather simple: White academics chose the literature they knew and that meshed best with their own cultural experiences. Hence, they institutionalized their own heritage and values for all who study literature. Actions that institutionalize a particular value present a challenge, however, to everyone who does not share in the cultural power. Consequently, there have been generations of non-White, non-Western European students of literature subjected to this canon without ever having the chance to read anything relevant to their own lives and heritage. Furthermore, White literature students miss out on the opportunity to study literature emanating from different cultures as they are led to believe that their heritage represents the bulk of valued thinking and writing.

My good colleague, Jamie Almanzan, relates how he never enjoyed a book he had to read in school until he was getting his master's degree in education at Stanford University. Jamie comes from a proud Latino heritage, and none of the literature he had ever studied considered this culture. A professor assigned the class *House on Mango Street* by Sandra Cisneros, a story of growing up Latina in the United States. It was revolutionary for Jamie. For the first time in his long academic career, he was reading a book that represented him and his heritage. Up to this point, the institutionalized literacy canon had served Jamie's cohorts in school very well, but it had never served him.

Dennis Littky, principal of the alternative high school mentioned earlier in this chapter, has achieved high success with low-income students and students of Color. In founding and directing the "Met" in Providence, Rhode Island, he deliberately challenged every aspect of the traditional high school. In Littky's (2004) book, *The Big Picture,* he describes the history of institutionalized education in the United States:

> In 1892, the National Education Association's (NEA) National Council formed the "Committee of 10." The president of Harvard University was the chair, and the other nine members were equally intellectual types from the elite institutions of the time. This tiny group set out to standardize high school programs on a national scale. They proclaimed exactly what subjects students should be taught, in what order, and even originated the concept of tracking, including stating that secondary education was only appropriate for a small portion of youth. (You can bet their *own* kids were included in that small portion.) . . . This "gang of 10," as I like to call them, also set in stone the idea that education is a one-size-fits-all institution. As the *Historical Dictionary of American Education* says, "The Committee asserted that every subject should be taught the same way to all pupils." . . . This is the archaic piece of paper that most schools still use, without even knowing it, as the basis for their rigid curricula and graduation requirements. (p. 29)

The "gang of 10" institutionalized their own value set as the model for all schools to follow. Few educators understand the historical origins of education as an institution. We collectively hold on to the mythologies of the public school system being built as the perpetuator of democracy and the pathway to social mobility. Rather, public education's origin was to create a minimally educated reliable workforce to serve the needs of the country's economic engine. Littky continues,

> Back in the industrial age, which is when our "modern" model of schooling was set up, the idea was that schools could churn out educated people much like factories churned out clothes and cars. . . . We've since gone from the industrial age to the information age. But even with huge changes like desegregation, New Math, and technology, nearly every classroom you walk into today looks just like the ones we all sat in, no matter our age. . . . Today, as yesterday, a traditional school is a building that isolates large groups of young people from adults and the resources and experiences of the real world, then expects them to emerge at 18 knowing how to be adult, how to work, and how to live in the real world. Society is asking our graduates for skills and fast-paced communication, and schools are still giving them facts and one-way lectures. Something is wrong here. (p. 30)

The very essence of public education has remained the same: an equal education for large aggregated groups of students. Without questioning the origin of our current educational system, it remains difficult to challenge the institution itself so that equity for all individual students can be actualized.

For a large institution like public education to change, it must come from within. Public education has a strong racist legacy and persistent inequities that must be addressed. I believe that most educational leaders, bureaucrats, and teachers have basic clean motives and moral purpose in what they do—they do not see themselves as the problem. The greatest challenge in equitizing schools lies in helping people to see the role they unconsciously play in the perpetuation of educational inequities. It is the institution itself that must be challenged—the collective of all members of the institution and their collective inequitable actions.

As equity becomes institutionalized, individuals within the school or school system become the force to address educational inequity. To challenge traditional institutionalism requires that the individuals within the institution collectively challenge long-standing values, assumption, beliefs, and especially the expectations as to who will and will not succeed predictably within the system. Without you, the individual, challenging your own institution, no change can occur.

DOMINANT CULTURE: WHITENESS

As the parents of two beautiful children who are Black, one of the hardest choices my wife and I face is where to send them to school. Just like most educational institutions, students of Color perform significantly worse than White students in our local school system. Statistically, we have no guarantee of presumed success in school for our children like both of us experienced. We essentially have two choices: send them to a primarily White school that is high performing where they will never look the norm, or to a low-performing school that is primarily students of Color where they will blend in. Already in their young age, our Black children are confronted with the White world of their parents. Society's Whiteness and racial inequities surround them.

My wife and I work extensively with White couples who have adopted children of Color. These couples clearly love their children, but the central theme of our work in transracial adoption states that *love is not enough.* In order to protect their children of Color, the parents need to understand racism and its impact on their children's lives. However, learning only about racism develops a limited understanding of the outward symptoms of the problem. These parents are raising children of Color in a very White world, and the all-consuming prevalence of White culture—termed *Whiteness*—is the empowering force behind the racism.

The challenge with Whiteness is that it so predominates our culture that its traits have become normed. As the norm, it remains unnamed. In *Cultural Proficiency,* Lindsey et al. (2003) write, "Dominant groups, the groups in power, do not name themselves; they name other people. The others are named in relationship to the dominant group" (p. 45). School systems tend not to address the inequities of "majority" or "White" or "wealthy" achievement, rather they address "minority," "Black," "Latino," and "poverty" student achievement—the group in privileged power remains unnamed while the *other* is labeled.

The power and privilege of White racial dominance allows this unnaming of Whiteness to occur. Henze et al. (2002, p. 9) present a formula that describes institutionalized racism—and ultimately institutionalized Whiteness:

Racism = racial prejudice + institutional power

Institutionalized racism occurs when one racial group comprehends its value set as being better than other racial groups' value sets, but then uses its societal power to enforce their values as the primary standards for everyone. As the predominant racial group in the United States, Whites have the power, and Whiteness persists as the cultural norm.

Exploring the nature of Whiteness while writing the first edition of *Courageous Conversations About Race,* my coauthor and mentor Glenn Singleton challenged me to consider my own assumptions of how society *should* work—what did I assume? What did I value? What did I see as the "right" thing to do? We summarized Whiteness in four distinct ways:

- *Individualism:* The belief set in White America that "it is all up to me," "I earned this," "pull yourself up by your boot straps," and other values which emphasize individual rights and actions above those of society.
- *Avoidance:* Primarily focusing on *my* life, *my* neighborhood, *my* belief set, and *my* own goodness at the expense of analyzing one's own role in institutionalized privilege and inequity: Since *I* did not cause racism, "It isn't my problem."
- *Decontextualization:* Depersonalizing inequity by intellectually analyzing what happens elsewhere and to others, rather than one's own situation. "How is it there?" becomes the question rather than "how is it here?"
- *Universal perspective:* An assumption that *my* understanding must be *the* understanding, and that varying viewpoints are likely due to another's lack of insight and knowledge, rather than just a different perspective. (Singleton & Linton, 2006, p. 192)

It is easy to dismiss these four characteristics as "universal" rather than "White" in nature. When I first heard these, they seemed so natural and obvious that it took me many years to see that individualism, avoidance, decontextualization, and universal perspective accurately reflect me and my White cultural background—I so exhibited these traits that they never seemed anything but natural.

To illustrate this, reflect back on a college literature class, and what the professor valued most in the discussion. When analyzing a book, did the professor honor the personal comment about how someone felt while reading the book? Or, did the professor most respect the analytical and intellectualized comments? I always knew how to make commentaries that professors loved—illustrate my *individual* intellect, *avoid* emotional connection to the subject, and *decontextualize* the topic into a *universal perspective*.

I have often seen in schools the prevalence of Whiteness. I once observed a White teacher approach a Latino boy sitting alone in her classroom. She knelt down and told him that she had been to Mexico over the summer. Mentioning that she had heard Mexicans pronounce the boy's last name in a different way than he himself pronounced it, she asked her American-born Latino student if he knew the "*correct* way to pronounce" his last name. The boy sat there with a blank face not knowing in any way how to respond to the teacher. Her Whiteness and his non-Whiteness were in direct conflict at this moment. She had individualized her own experience as more important than her student's. She avoided the fact that he grew up in the United States. She decontextualized his current and local reality by placing his life in another country thousands of miles away. And, she processed his last name through a lens of universal perspective, thus invalidating his unique and personal existence as represented by his name. The teacher was only trying to make a personal connection, but in exhibiting her Whiteness, she managed to distance herself from the student because of her unintentional lack of respect toward his personal diversity.

INSTITUTIONALIZED WHITENESS

Long before I had ever heard of Whiteness, I had learned well from society how to live it. Not all White people necessarily exhibit these characteristics, while many people of Color do. My wife, who is White, rarely made a comment in college because she reflects naturally in a very personal and emotional way. But, she felt subconsciously the *presence* of Whiteness and the value the institution placed on its characteristics since she was constantly self-conscious of being quiet in class. Even though she went to a college with over 50 percent students of Color, White cultural characteristics predominated at her university. Likewise, most educators of Color learn how to value and exhibit the traits of Whiteness in order to survive education's very White institutions. In schools, *institutionalized Whiteness* is a dominant cultural force that excludes others' full and equal participation.

But as a White person, if I am conscious of my racial privilege and actively challenge racism, am I still responsible for Whiteness? Yes, because Whiteness is tied first to the power of the institution, not just the individual. The difficulty with institutionalized Whiteness is that it requires each of us to accept our own position of power and privilege within the institution. Singleton and I write in *Courageous Conversations About Race:*

> Racism becomes institutionalized when organizations—such as a school or school district—remain unconscious of issues related to race or more actively perpetuate and enforce a dominant racial perspective or belief . . . institutionalized racism persists in American culture and its educational systems due to educators' inaction as well as actions considered harmful to students of Color. To serve students of Color equitably, it is essential to challenge institutionalized racism. (Singleton & Linton, 2006, p. 41)

Simply addressing individual racist acts will never overcome institutionalized discrimination. To break down inequities, we must directly challenge the system.

I once documented a Southern California high school math team that deliberately challenged the institutionalized prejudice apparent in their operations. The school had set the policy that any student scoring in the top quartile on the previous year's exam would be placed in advanced math. In this school that was evenly split between White, Asian, Black, and Latino students, the teachers assumed the policy was being followed. All of their advanced math classes, however, were almost exclusively White and Asian. This meant that either White and Asian students were more capable, or that an inequity existed.

To address this, the team courageously aligned performance on the previous year's exam with class placement. What they discovered was gross inequity: all Asian and White students who scored in the top quartile were in advanced math, whereas only half of the Black students and a couple of Latino students scoring in the top quartile were actually placed in advanced math. Looking at the second quartile of performance, almost 100 percent of Asian students and nearly 90 percent of White students were in advanced math, whereas only a few Black students and no Latino students scoring in the second quartile were in advanced math. This greatly disturbed the math team. Because of the school's inconsistent policy enforcement, great institutional inequities persisted. This exercise allowed the math team to honestly address biases they themselves had exhibited and begin building institutionalized equity.

Singleton and I further wrote,

> Rarely is intentional discrimination the central problem in the teacher-student relationship; rather, the discrimination includes unquestioned assumptions on the part of the institution within which these interactions take place. These assumptions—such as Asian students are better at math, Latino parents don't support their kids in school, or advanced placement classes are too difficult for Black students—are at the heart of the racial achievement gap. Thus, institutionalized racism means to allow these negative assumptions to persist unchallenged by those having positional power. Unquestioned assumptions about the attitudes and abilities of students of Color and their families are the basis for detrimental instructional practices that foster and preserve racial inequities in schools. (Singleton & Linton, 2006, p. 42)

As I personally challenge institutionalized Whiteness, I challenge not only the power structures that I am part of, but I challenge my own set of assumptions and perceptions of the world and how it operates. To accomplish equity in schools, educators need to heighten their consciousness of Whiteness and its associated norms. In doing this, schools will successfully engage diverse students simply as they are versus how well they relate to the school's traditional norms.

WHO EQUITABLY BENEFITS?

Culturally, equitable school systems implement the practice of always asking, "Who equitably benefits?" By institutionalizing this habit, educators keep the focus on individually serving the needs of each student. This question, then, needs to be asked of every policy, program, and practice:

- Who equitably benefits from our curriculum decisions?
- Who equitably benefits from our teacher hiring and assignments?
- Who equitably benefits from our gifted, honors, and AP programs?
- Who equitably benefits from our special education and RTI programs?
- Who equitably benefits from our extracurricular activities?
- Who equitably benefits from our budget decisions?
- Who equitably benefits from our accountability measures?
- Who equitably benefits from our learning goals?

Without inserting equity language into the question as to who benefits from decisions and programs within the school or system, educators are not forced to consider whether or not the effort individually serves the learning needs of all students in pursuit of meeting or exceeding a common standard, regardless of race, ethnicity, culture, gender, socioeconomics, and language.

As equity becomes institutionalized, the benefits are numerous, especially for students in their learning. In *The Right to Learn,* Linda Darling-Hammond (1997) describes the beneficial outcomes of restructuring how a school functions:

Restructured schools produce high achievement with more students of all abilities and graduate more of them with better levels of skills and understanding than traditional schools do. We now know much about what schools structured for success look like. They organize teachers' and students' work together in ways that get beyond bureaucracy to produce:

- Active in-depth learning
- Emphasis on authentic performance

- Attention to development
- Appreciation for diversity
- Opportunities for collaborative learning
- A collective perspective across the school
- Structures for caring
- Support for democratic learning
- Connections to family and community (p. 64)

INSTITUTIONALIZED EQUITY EQUALS PERSISTENCE

For a school system to succeed at equity, all parts—from top administrators to classroom teachers—need to be focused on the same objectives and goals. Likewise, policies, practices, and procedures need to align with equity. With this collective synergy, the efforts will last long enough for true change to succeed. Consequently, the prevailing characteristic of institutionalized equity is persistence.

Equity is realized when the institution itself becomes equitable. To reiterate, *institutionalized equity* is:

Institutionalized policies, processes, and practices that guarantee educators provide all students with the individual support they need to reach and exceed a common standard or expectation.

Well-executed, classroom-level practice follows systemic policy. If the institutional focus on equity remains consistent, support is pervasive, goals are clear, and educators are held collectively responsible for student achievement, systemwide persistence toward equity can occur.

Institutionalizing equity has clear results, as evidenced in the success stories presented in this book, and in substantial research that exists on how schools turn around. The practices have been outlined in numerous books and publications. My own company, the School Improvement Network, has documented on video hundreds of successful teaching examples. The proof is clear as to what schools can accomplish, and how they can do it. The difference is in the will of the school and school system to collectively implement equitable practices with all educators.

As evidenced in the school success stories shared so far, equity is always a multiple-year effort. Because of this, equitable leaders need to be keenly aware of challenges along the way. Linda Darling-Hammond (1997) writes,

> The amount of effort and influence required to change a school system policy is so great that most teachers, principals, and parents find it impossible to deflect enough energies from their primary jobs to the arduous and often unrewarding task of moving the behemoth. Over time cynicism overwhelms problem solving, and the pressures for conformity become so strong that most principals and teachers are afraid to test the limits of the system. (p. 67)

But when a school system changes its limits, success becomes tangible. In Sanger Unified School District, their persistence in building institutional equity is paying off, for adults and students alike. As described by the superintendent, Marc Johnson,

> Typically in the past at the end of the year, I would approach a teacher and ask them, "So how are you doing?" "Oh, it's been a long year and I am really looking forward to summer." In the last three years, I can honestly say that I have not had a teacher say that. What they say is, "You know, it has been a long year, but let me tell you what we are going to do next year, Marc." And they begin to share their conversations with their peers about their plan for next year. At that point where typically it is the lowest energy point of the year, May coming into June, where they have run hard and they are tired, there is still enthusiasm and excitement about the work to come. Those are the sort of things that let you know *it's a different place!*

EQUITY IN ACTION: CHAPTER 5, INSTITUTIONAL EQUITY

Equity Discussion

In a group, discuss the definition of *institutionalized equity:*

Institutionalized policies, processes, and practices that guarantee educators provide all students with the individual support they need to reach and exceed a common standard or expectation.

In what ways does your institution exhibit policies, processes, and practices that enable equity? What role can be played by individual educators to influence the institution's equity efforts? How equitable is your institution?

EQUITY LENS: INSTITUTIONAL

The following exercise serves two purposes: (1) to help you analyze the degree to which your school or school system is equitable, and (2) to distinguish the difference between an equitable and inequitable educational institution. I first learned about the educational and analytical power of a sliding scale poll from Ruth Johnson (2002), author of *Using Data to Close the Achievement Gap,* a book wherein she provides numerous analytical tools to help understand institutionalized inequities.

Institutional Equity Poll

In the polls below, quickly determine the approximate percentage of students, teachers, and administrators who match the *equitable* example on the right. To contrast the characteristic, the *inequitable* example is stated on the left. For example, on the question about student relationships with teachers, roughly calculate the percent of students who have a good relationship with a teacher. Do not over-think your responses, as this is meant primarily for reflection on the equity of your school and/or system.

Student Equity

Inequity	← Sliding Scale →					Equity
Students do not have strong relationships with educators.	20%	40%	60%	80%	100%	Students have one or more meaningful relationships with an educator.
Students do not feel that the school values their culture, race, and background.	20%	40%	60%	80%	100%	Students believe that the school values their culture, race, and background.
Students do not feel the school has high expectations of them.	20%	40%	60%	80%	100%	Students understand the high learning expectations the school has for them.

(Continued)

(Continued)

Inequity	←	*Sliding Scale*	→			Equity
School has no relation or communication with parents and community.	20%	40%	60%	80%	100%	School has strong relationships and collaboration with parents and community.
Students are not individually supported in their learning needs.	20%	40%	60%	80%	100%	Students are individually supported in their learning needs and in who they are.

Teacher Classroom Equity

Inequity	←	*Sliding Scale*	→			Equity
Teachers do not understand students' race, ethnicity, and culture.	20%	40%	60%	80%	100%	Teachers understand students racially, culturally, and ethnically.
Teachers gear all instruction to the whole classroom.	20%	40%	60%	80%	100%	Teachers instruct, support, and connect with each student individually.
Teachers only use traditional instructional methods.	20%	40%	60%	80%	100%	Teachers differentiate instruction with best practices and strategies.
Teachers work in isolation and minimally rely upon school support.	20%	40%	60%	80%	100%	Teachers collaborate and rely upon support structures to improve teaching and learning.
Teachers use an unaligned curriculum that is not culturally relevant for students.	20%	40%	60%	80%	100%	Teachers rigorously instruct the standards in a culturally relevant way.

Leadership Equity

Inequity	← Sliding Scale →					Equity
Leadership does not recognize or honor the diversity of students.	20%	40%	60%	80%	100%	Leadership respects the diversity of students and addresses inequities.
School leaders provide only required professional development.	20%	40%	60%	80%	100%	School leaders direct dynamic professional development that is job embedded and tied to teacher needs.
The school/system's vision, mission, values, and policies are not equitable for all.	20%	40%	60%	80%	100%	The school/system's vision, mission, values, and policies drive institutional equity.
The school/system does not achieve performance goals for students.	20%	40%	60%	80%	100%	The school/system consistently reaches and exceeds learning goals for every student.
Administrators and teachers are not held accountable for poor student achievement.	20%	40%	60%	80%	100%	Administrators and teachers are personally accountable for student learning and achievement.

EQUITY ACTION #5

Based on your institutional equity poll, describe your institution according to equity. How equitable is your institution, its practices, policies, beliefs, and cultural understandings? For students? Teachers? Leaders? What impact has this had on student achievement?

Share your poll and analysis with a colleague and/or administrator.

Deepening Equity: Institutional Reflection

Analyze your school and/or school system according to the institutionalized Whiteness characteristics:

- Individualism
- Avoidance
- Decontextualization
- Universal perspective

How are these characteristics exhibited in your institution in terms of leadership, culture, and practice? What impact do these have upon the academic success of students, especially those from diverse backgrounds? What impact do these have upon the ability of the school or system to change and improve?

CHAPTER 6

Professional Equity

A friend's mother once described being a professional as "getting paid for what you like to do." Of all professional fields, education surely has one of the highest percentages of workers who entered the field for the satisfaction of the work, and not just the paycheck or recognition. But teaching, and leading teachers, is simply hard work—endless, thankless, criticized, and stressful. Being an educator need not be fraught with frustration, for with success comes satisfaction—and in an equitable school where all students are at grade level and above, this success fulfills the aspirations most educators had for entering education in the first place: to change the life of a child.

To accomplish equity, educators must work at the personal, institutional, and professional levels. Personal equity poses the question, who am I? Institutional equity explores, who are we? Professional equity addresses the logical next question, what do we do to build equity for all students?

The focus of *professional equity* is on the teaching practices, support mechanisms, and environment that actualize equity. So much of traditional professional development has focused on the skills of teaching that the personal and institutional have usually remained unexamined. But when the implementation of equity is the focus of an educational institution and its educators, the "effective strategies," "best practices," and "professional learning" of a school are contextualized within the overarching objective of serving the learning needs of each and every student. With professional equity, pedagogically sound practice takes root and flourishes because the objective is clear: the academic success of every individual student, no matter their race, ethnicity, culture, socioeconomic status, gender, and language.

Numerous books and resources provide examples of schools that have eliminated achievement inequities and lifted all students to high levels of learning. The Education Trust's Karin Chenoweth (2007) opens her book, *"It's Being Done:" Academic Success in Unexpected Schools,* with the big question:

> Can it be done? Can schools help all children learn to high levels, even poor children and children of Color? Is it even possible for schools to help children who face the substantial obstacles of poverty and discrimination to learn to read, write, compute, and generally become educated citizens? (p. 1)

Chenoweth then goes on to describe how fifteen schools at all levels eliminated their academic inequities on the path toward high achievement. Throughout her book, the obvious answer to the question of whether it can be done is a resounding yes!

Students rely upon the educators and leaders within their schools to change their practices so that they can succeed. With a committed staff, persistent leadership, and successful implementation of equity, any school can succeed with any student. Without equitizing today's schools, what are our students' futures?

EQUITY SUCCESS: DUNBAR HIGH SCHOOL

Seven years ago, principal Roger Shaw and assistant principal Stephen Colbert were leading Paul Laurence Dunbar High School in Baltimore, Maryland—a school in crisis and on the verge of state takeover due to perennial low performance. It was a magnet school with no magnetizing effect upon students. Enrollment was down, student achievement was abysmal, and already low graduation rates were slipping further.

Dunbar had dedicated educators—they worked hard and cared about their students. But, there was no clear vision of what the school should look like, nor direction as to where the school should go.

Excellence was lacking. In a school where 95 percent of the students are Black, and over half the students are from poverty, Dunbar was supposed to provide these students with a promising future. According to current principal, Stephen Colbert, "We had an urgent need to really transform our program so that we could meet these state achievement requirements."

From the crisis of an impending state takeover, the educators at Dunbar embraced change and intensified their professional efforts in building a culture of excellence where all students can—and will—succeed. Preparing for graduation, senior Joshua Melton describes how Dunbar taught him about success, "Excellence isn't always about winning or losing. It's about your pursuit of the win and loss." Dunbar High now empowers its students to pursue their dreams by taking risks in the pursuit of excellence. This pursuit of excellence has led to the phenomenal graduation rate of 100 percent of all students. Not a single student is lost on the path to graduation. This is the guarantee of equity—all students receive the individual support they need to reach and ultimately exceed the standard.

"We made a turn around just at the right time," explains Stephen. "The year they were about to implement the school improvement program, we met AYP [annual yearly progress], and we haven't missed it since." The school leadership looked nationally for models that could work at Dunbar. Teachers were willing to collaborate before the changes, but there had been no formal process. In its pursuit of excellence, Dunbar embraced professional learning communities.

These efforts led to a significant increase in the support teachers received, not only from leadership, but also from each other. Math teacher Lindsay Clifton describes the mentoring new teachers receive, "You have a mentor teacher. You have Mr. Shaw or Mr. Colbert coming in and checking on you saying, 'Can I help you out?' 'How's it going?' 'Let me observe you,' and give you little tidbits."

The administration visits multiple classrooms daily and provides immediate instructional feedback to teachers. Math teacher and robotics coach Lawrence Totty explains, "That gives you a chance to grow, a chance to meet the standards not just for the school, but for the other staff. You sort of pick up the good habits that the other teachers have."

Dunbar High School administration developed professionalism among its educators by focusing on the individual strengths and weaknesses of each teacher. Raquel Smith, head of the social studies department, says, "We have good administrators who are well prepared. They are concerned about people first because you have to be concerned about the whole person, the whole student. Then the person's educational status will automatically follow and improve." In their professional development, teachers learn in much the same way that students are treated in their learning—teachers are allowed to explore, collaborate with colleagues, share, and expected to grow continuously toward excellence in their practice.

Excellence has become the norm at Dunbar: "When you see how many teachers do other things, when you see how many teachers do more than just the eight to three—that's the bare minimum," explains Lawrence. "And that is exactly what Dunbar is not about; Dunbar is about much more than the bare minimum. The bare minimum is not accepted here."

One of Dunbar's first innovations was "Saturday Academy," wherein the school opened on weekends so students could come to receive extra assistance in mathematics. Stephen explains, "We were amazed on the first day of the Saturday Academy. Almost 80 percent of our math students were there."

Lindsay remarks on the students' embrace of the additional one-on-one instructional assistance: "We encouraged everyone to come," she explains. "We were here. Administration was here. We had close to a hundred kids on Saturdays."

After the students knew the school was serious about helping them succeed academically, the students responded in kind by taking advantage of all the support offered by the school. Prior to Saturday Academy, only 16 percent of Dunbar's students passed the state math exam. In that first year, math scores went up to 43 percent—and, math scores have steadily climbed ever since.

According to Stephen, "We have a wrap-around type of support. We take kids where they are. When they come in the door, whatever baggage they have, we take them, and we begin to unpack them." The Dunbar staff provides a nurturing environment for students so that they can focus on building their own academic success. As teacher Euodias Parker describes, "We like students to know who they are and teach them how to turn a negative situation in to a positive situation."

Dunbar balances the academic support for students with the emotional support they also need. The teachers are well aware of students' needs, whatever they may be. Lawrence explains, "During this high school time, [students] are going to feel some periods of isolation . . . when [they] are surrounded by faculty that care, administrators that care, [they succeed]."

This student support begins with the well-ingrained belief that the students are capable of remarkable achievement. Raquel says that, "We recognize that they are all geniuses. And so when they come here, we accept them, and we teach them that 'you may not be in an AP class, but we're going to teach you like you're AP.'"

Dunbar hosts a nationally ranked robotics team that engages students and provides them another opportunity to achieve excellence. This team is known in the robotic world as the "Lab Rats." They recently placed fourteenth at the high school world robotics championship. Senior Dominique Douglas describes what the team has done for her: "It's not so much about the winning, it's being part of a team—it's like a family, you can go and talk to any one of the teammates about anything."

As the robotics coach, Lawrence grants the students significant autonomy in their robotics projects to help them take more ownership in their effort and success. "The kids embrace it and find identity in it. It's a lot of work, but it is still a family-type structure." From a student perspective, Dominique adds, "With the mentors and friends I've made, it's extreme. It's something I'm extremely happy for. It made me who I am today. I have potential to be something greater."

At Dunbar High, the students are well aware of the life lessons taught by teachers at all times, whether in the classroom, on teams, or in the hallway. The goal of equity is readily apparent because students are focused on academic and extracurricular successes that collectively prepare them for life beyond high school. According to senior Jasmin Johnson, "It teaches you stuff you need in the real world, like time management, how to deal with all these attitudes, dedication, putting forth the work if you want to get something done."

Business and technology teacher Sandra Johnson further explains, "I have learned so many useful techniques to use with my students. We're firm. We're consistent. We always expect them to reach the highest level. But, they know that we care. We're genuine about the way we feel about our students." She concludes, "Our students are achievers. They strive for success. We want them to succeed. That's why we're here."

Success is readily apparent at Dunbar High School. It has achieved what high schools almost never accomplish—all students performing at grade level. In the seventh year of their change process, Dunbar achieved the seemingly impossible:

- 100 percent passing math high school assessment
- 100 percent passing biology high school assessment
- 100 percent passing English high school assessment
- 100 percent passing social studies high school assessment

Every student in this diverse high school performed at grade level. Even more remarkable than the academic performance is what happens to Dunbar students at the end of high school:

- 100 percent graduation rate
- 100 percent college bound

Thankful for his Dunbar education, senior Joshua Melton explains how the atmosphere helps everyone strive to be better: "My coaches always say that it is hard for you to not want to be great when everybody around you wants to be great. . . . We push each other to be better, and don't even know it!"

The following equity lens for Dunbar High illustrates how the school institutionalized equity for all students. They have been deliberate and balanced in their improvement efforts in the areas of culture, practice, and leadership.

Dunbar truly fulfills the aim of equity—individually serving each student to reach and exceed a common standard. As I left Dunbar High, I complimented the principal on the remarkable work he and the staff have done. I also mentioned to him how his was a high school where I would willingly send my children. He thanked me and asked, "Why?" My response was, "Because you are *guaranteeing* success for every student. It is not a promise, it's guaranteed!"

Figure 6.1 Equity Lens: Dunbar High School

CULTURE

Personal Strategies

- Expect educators to build relationships with students.
- Support students one-on-one to see their own potential.

Institutional Strategies

- Create academies throughout school so that students and teachers know each other well.
- Support extracurricular activities for wide range of student interest, such as robotics.

Professional Strategies

- Schedule and support PLC collaboration.
- Empower teachers to understand student learning needs.

PRACTICE

Personal Strategies

- Individually analyze and develop pedagogical practices of teachers.
- Expect teachers to master instructional strategies.

Institutional Strategies

- Provide professional development that models strategies across the school.
- Create extra learning opportunities, such as Saturday Academy.

Professional Strategies

- Provide techniques for differentiating the instruction.
- Share effective pedagogical practices in teams and across grade levels.

EQUITY

LEADERSHIP

Personal Strategies

- Self-evaluate educators' own academic expectations of students.
- Internalize meaning of student success.

Institutional Strategies

- Reinforce emphasis on improving instructional practice throughout school.
- Empower department heads to drive reform efforts.

Professional Strategies

- Use data systematized throughout school to drive instruction.
- Establish collective responsibility to support every student in their individual learning needs.

SHIFTING PRACTICE

How can a school or school system replicate the success of Dunbar High School, Frankford Elementary, Sanger Unified School District, or any other highly diverse educational institution that has erased its achievement disparity and provided all students with an equitable education? There is no clear and definitive approach or strategy, nor expert who has the precise answer. Every school I have studied that has eliminated its achievement inequities did it in its own unique way. There are commonalities, however, and frameworks to apply that can guide a school in developing its own authentic path to equity.

Despite the constant barrage of criticism, I have witnessed a great shift in educational equity since the passage of No Child Left Behind (NCLB). It is by no means perfect legislation, but it forced educators to deeply examine their practices and choose to either address their achievement issues or accept the label of a failing school. With NCLB, all schools now disaggregate their data, thus exposing unmistakable achievement gaps between certain student groups. Without question, this pressure surfaced significant bad practice in some schools when they became too focused on AYP. But every year, I see more and more examples of schools that are closing their gaps authentically and successfully. The crises created by AYP requirements have just as often led schools to innovate, focus, and change their behaviors in order to better succeed with all students.

PRACTICE TO THEORY

Most of what I know about how to accomplish equity in schools comes from the insight of colleagues. Bonnie Davis, my coauthor on the *Equity 101 Culture* book, is truly a teacher's teacher—she loves the profession, and is passionate about how the work can improve. Most beneficial in my conversations with her is that she always turns it back to what teachers are actually doing successfully in the class-room. She derives her understanding of educational theory from the actual practices of successful educators.

The best educational changes come from observing and learning from other education practitioners, and then reflecting on one's own practice. There is no need to reinvent the wheel since there is already a wheel that works—it's just that not everyone knows how to make it roll. To learn from another's practice requires great diligence because educators are typically less proficient in this form of professional learning. Traditionally, educators sit and listen to someone explain what they should be doing, and then they might observe a teacher demonstrate a model lesson in their own classroom. But change and progress arise from messy reality, not the perfect presentation.

I recently completed an extensive project with Michael Fullan (2010) documenting school systems engaged in *Motion Leadership,* which is quick and simple change processes aimed at getting immediate movement toward school improvement goals. In observing these schools, he drove a concept I had often pondered: *practice to theory.* By focusing first on the practitioner, we can ground our improvement efforts in actuality, rather than in ideality. In comparison to traditional school improvement efforts, this approach is quite radical because it places the focus on ground-level educators who have already succeeded rather than on the researcher or "expert" theoretician. Instead of developing a good idea and then figuring out how to apply it, educators need to identify the successful approaches already working in schools, and then figure out how to widely replicate them.

In one correspondence about practice to theory, Michael sent me the following e-mail:

> Practice is way more liberating than theory. Thus we will honor and push practice to discover its own potential. It is: practice to theory; practice to evidence; practice to research. No more looking for answers in the wrong places and wrong starting points. Practitioners don't need to be dependent on theory, researchers, management gurus and the like. We want them to exercise their own futures. (personal communication, December 9, 2009)

Profound in its simplicity, practice to theory can dramatically change the way educational leaders approach school improvement. Rather than finding a great external idea, a principal seeks out a teacher within the school or one nearby who has helped all students succeed, studies how that teacher instructs and works with students, and then focuses professional development on replicating that localized successful practice with the entire staff. Likewise, a superintendent can identify the most successful principal in the system or in a system nearby, study how that principal has increased student achievement throughout the school, and then incorporate those practices throughout every school in the system.

This approach shows deep professional respect to educators. It reinforces that professional educators are fully capable of their own success—they are responsible for their *own* change efforts, can direct their own learning, guide themselves toward their own improvement, and act decisively as a true professional. At the end of the e-mail, Michael added a quote by Samuel Johnson: "All theory is against the freedom of the will; all experience is for it."

In *"It's Being Done,"* Karin Chenoweth (2007) applies practice to theory in her research on highly successful diverse schools. Focusing first on practice as the basis of theory opened up an exciting world of educational possibility:

> I began this project not knowing at all what I would find. I was identifying schools solely on the basis of their student achievement test scores, and for all I knew (and feared), I would find the soul-deadening test-prep factories that we are told characterize high-poverty and high-minority schools that do well on state assessments . . . I found none of that. Instead I found dedicated, energetic, skilled professionals who talk about the needs of children and who care deeply about whether all their students have access to the kinds of knowledge and opportunities that most middle-class White children take for granted. That means that they care about and include in their teaching art and music and physical fitness and field trips and science and history and all the things that some people say must be cut out of schools in order to focus on the reading and math skills tested in state assessments. That doesn't mean that the people in the schools I have visited don't care deeply about reading and math and about doing well on state assessments, but they know that it is a mistake to "narrow the curriculum" and "teach to the test"—two of the epithets that are floating around the education world. And, happily, I found teachers and principals who love their jobs. They work hard, and some work long hours. . . . Many are bolstered by the idea that they are engaged in important work—work that, if enough people paid attention, could improve the teaching profession and to some extent the nation itself. (p. 3)

EQUITIZING STANDARDS

The goal of educational equity is measurable success for every student:

> Educators provide all students with the individualized support they need to reach and exceed a common standard.

But within this definition of educational equity is an apparent paradox: "individually support" and "common standard"—the former is about the power of the individual whereas the latter is about the power of the collective. This goes back to the fundamental difference between an *equal* school system and an *equitable* school system. In an equal school system, all students get "equal access" to the entrance, which assumes that all students are showing up equally prepared to learn. An equitable school system recognizes that this is not the case, and individualizes the instruction based on each student's needs so that all students can succeed. Likewise, the measurement of a common standard for all students guides each one of them toward reaching some degree of equality of achievement at the exit, thus allowing all students to have equal opportunity moving from school into the world beyond.

Numerous proven strategies exist to facilitate individualizing the learning for each student, such as differentiated instruction, project-based learning, constructivism, and teaching for mastery. According to Charlotte Danielson (2007),

> Fundamentally, learning is done by individuals, not by groups. So although it is essential for a teacher to know that some students in the class learn quickly, or that another group of individuals does not understand a particular concept, the knowledge of group needs is only a compilation of the knowledge of individual characteristics. (p. 35)

The research about standards has been equally compelling and significant, resulting in the recent issuance of the Common Core State Standards, which will serve as college- and career-readiness standards in the vast majority of U.S. states. These standards are significant in terms of equity because they establish a national measuring stick; this will (1) allow all teachers and students to know exactly what they are supposed to learn, and (2) pinpoint precisely where inequities in instruction exist based on student performance.

Currently, one of the most successful large school systems is in the province of Ontario, Canada. Ontario has aggressively converted their use of standards and the assessments that follow into formative assessment tools for schools and educators. According to Eleanor Newman, senior executive officer at the Ontario Ministry of Education in Toronto, Ontario, "We asked a different question. Instead of saying, 'What is the work telling us about how the students are doing?' we asked the question, 'What is the student's work telling us about how we are doing?'" (as cited in Fullan, 2010).

By establishing a common standard, school systems shift the focus from time spent on teaching to the actual learning that occurs. According to standards and accountability expert Doug Reeves (1996),

> The learning expectation must be fixed—children will learn to add and subtract. The time it takes to learn this may be shorter for some children and longer for others, but it is not acceptable that "some kids just won't learn it." At the very heart of the standards movements is the change from fixed time, variable learning, to variable amounts of time to learn with fixed standards for learning. (p. 19)

Reeves goes on to illustrate this with the "standards of performance" that all athletes clearly understand: "It is not coincidental that in our most standards-based endeavor—athletics, where the benchmarks are clear and the standards widely understood—the barriers of race and socioeconomic status have been most easily broken" (p. 27).

In competitions, spectators could easily measure the difference in performance of Black athletes Jesse Owens and Jackie Robinson, thus breaking preconceived notions of ability tied to race. The same need for consistent expectations impacts diverse students within a school. Without a common standard for all students, learning failures are attributed to outside factors, such as poverty and race, thus excusing the school for its poor performance with certain student groups.

With standards, the need for individualized instruction becomes readily apparent. "A standards-based approach would begin and end with one question—what must students know and be able to do?" Reeves continues, "Then curriculum, assessment, and time requirements would be based on the answer to that question—an answer, by the way, that might be different for different students" (p. 29). When measuring each student against a common standard, an equitable school readily sees the ways in which individual students need to be taught and supported.

IMPLEMENTING EQUITY

Efforts to improve education are not new. Equity-driven efforts, however, are distinctive in that educators now focus on implementing success by individualizing student support. The Equity Framework provides guidance to educators working on equitizing their school or system for the benefit of all students. As individual educators see the purpose of improvement efforts, their localized support and enthusiasm become the sustaining force needed to accomplish equity.

In a study conducted by Linda Darling-Hammond and Arthur Wise, investigating why teachers might leave the profession, the most common answer was the use of a prescribed curriculum and teaching methods that might "render them ineffective and eliminate the remaining joys of teaching," rather than "low salaries, poor working conditions, student misbehavior, or lack of funding" (Darling-Hammond, 1997, p. 38). The enthusiasm and dedication of an educator is directly proportional to the potential impact that the educator feels possible with the students within the classroom or school. This is a practical issue within school improvement efforts: day-to-day professional efficacy engages and sustains educators through the challenges of implementing equity within a school.

In using the Equity Framework, the institution focuses holistically on obtaining equity by improving leadership, culture, and practice. By organizing strategies within a framework, obstacles and resistance have less impact on systemic equity reform. Engagement in the totality of this effort by all within the institution helps avoid derailment often caused by unforeseen issues in equity work.

In *Failure Is Not an Option,* Alan Blankstein (2004) illustrates a school, Kate Sullivan Elementary, that overcame its barriers by focusing on six principles critical to their success:

1. Establishing a common mission, vision, values, and goals

2. Ensuring achievement for all students: systems for prevention and intervention

3. Forming collaborative teaming focused on teaching and learning

4. Using data to guide decision making and continuous improvement

5. Gaining active engagement from family and community

6. Building sustainable leadership capacity (pp. 40–47)

Even though many school improvement approaches differ somewhat from each other, each of them succeeds in schools where they are implemented with fidelity. The Equity Framework is compatible with multiple school improvement approaches as it provides the context for the organization, support, and characteristics necessary for equity to take root and succeed with all students.

In *"It's Being Done,"* Chenoweth (2007) sums up the practices of the fifteen featured highly successful diverse schools:

- They teach their students.
- They don't teach to the state tests.
- They have high expectations for their students.
- They know what the stakes are.
- They embrace and use all the data they can get their hands on.
- They use data to focus on individual students, not just groups of students.
- They constantly reexamine what they do.
- They embrace accountability.
- They make decisions on what is good for kids, not what is good for adults.
- They use school time wisely.
- They leverage as many resources from the community as possible.
- They expand the time students—particularly struggling students—have in school.
- They do not spend a lot of time disciplining students, in the sense of punishing them.

- They establish an atmosphere of respect.
- They like kids.
- They make sure that the kids who struggle the most have the best instruction.
- Principals are a constant presence.
- Although the principals are important leaders, they are not the only leaders.
- They pay careful attention to the quality of the teaching staff.
- They provide teachers with the time to meet to plan and work collaboratively.
- They provide teachers time to observe each other.
- They think seriously about professional development.
- They assume that they will have to train new teachers more or less from scratch and carefully acculturate all newly hired teachers.
- They have high-quality, dedicated, and competent office and building staff who feel themselves part of the educational mission of the school.
- They are nice places to work. (pp. 216–226)

To sum up, because the educators in these schools expect their students to learn, they work hard to master the skills and knowledge necessary to teach those students.

An equitable school is both the right of your students and the responsibility of you and your colleagues. As exhibited throughout this book, the benefits of realizing equity within your school or system are numerous and powerful. But as educational professionals, equitizing your school is up to you and your institution.

EQUITY IN ACTION: CHAPTER 6, PROFESSIONAL EQUITY

Equity Discussion

As a group, discuss the intersection of professionalism and equity. What responsibilities do you hold as professional educators according to equity? How is an equitable school environment more rewarding professionally? What will it take to implement equity in your school and/or school system?

The Equity Framework serves as an analytical tool for determining whether your professional practices are equitable or not. The following equity lens is a multistep process that can be accomplished both formally and informally. To understand the purpose of this analysis, engage in it on your own informally, and then arrange time to do this analysis formally with colleagues. When done collaboratively, this process creates productive and honest dialogue as to whether individual practices and programs are equitable for all students. The goal is not just to identify the *equitable* things happening in your school or system, but rather whether or not all that you are currently doing leads to *equity.*

Part 1: Equity Framework Time and Resources

Roughly determine the percentage of *time* and *resources* (funds and staff) you spend in your total school improvement efforts addressing the three areas of the Equity Framework (totals between culture, practice, and leadership should equal 100 percent in time and 100 percent in resources):

- *Culture*—As a percentage of total school improvement efforts, how much time and resources are spent in building an effective learning culture where students and teachers alike are in a safe learning environment, collaboration is supported, and effort is spent developing cultural competency wherein the educators learn about the culture of themselves and their students?

  Culture time: _____%   Culture resources: _____%

- *Practice*—As a percentage of total school improvement efforts, how much time and resources are spent developing the pedagogical skills of teachers and helping them implement effective learning strategies, curriculum alignment and approaches, assessment methods, classroom management, interventions, and general teaching skills?

  Practice time: _____%   Practice resources: _____%

- *Leadership*—As a percentage of total school improvement efforts, how much time and resources are spent developing vision, direction, and accountability as well as improving the effectiveness, skills, and instructional leadership of administrators, support staff, and teacher leaders?

  Leadership time: _____%   Leadership resources: _____%

Part 2: School Improvement Programs, Initiatives, Efforts, Curriculum, and Professional Development

Using the form on page 130, complete the following exercises:

1. In the first column, list all school and teacher improvement programs, initiatives, and professional development efforts engaged in by your school and/or school system. It is critical to include everything you do in order to accurately understand your improvement efforts. This could include PLCs, RTI, "courageous conversations about race," leadership development, differentiation, coaching, curriculum support— anything administrators and teachers engage in to improve the school and classroom teaching.

2. In the second through fifth columns, analyze each item you listed according to expectations, rigor, relevancy, and relationships. Place a plus sign (+), check mark (✓), or minus sign (−) in each category based upon whether or not the program, initiative, curriculum, or professional development effort:

   + = supports high expectations, a rigorous curriculum, culturally relevant instruction, and/or strong student-educator relationships.

   ✓ = somewhat supports high expectations, a rigorous curriculum, culturally relevant instruction, and/or strong student-educator relationships.

   − = does not support high expectations, a rigorous curriculum, culturally relevant instruction, and/or strong student-educator relationships.

3. In the last column, determine if each school improvement program, initiative, curriculum, and professional development effort that you listed has been designed, analyzed, and implemented through the lens of equity by asking explicitly or implicitly "who equitably benefits?" Place a plus sign (+), check mark (✓), or minus sign (−) in the box based upon whether the item:

+ = achieves equity for all students, regardless of race, ethnicity, culture, socioeconomics, and language.

✓ = somewhat achieves equity for all students, regardless of race, ethnicity, culture, socioeconomics, and language.

− = does not achieve equity for all students, regardless of race, ethnicity, culture, socioeconomics, and language.

School and/or system improvement programs, initiatives, curriculum, and professional development	Supports high expectations +✓–	Provides rigorous learning +✓–	Relevant to students' lives and culture +✓–	Develops strong relationships +✓–	Who equitably benefits? +✓–
Sample: Professional development on differentiating instruction	+	+	✓	✓	+
1.					
2.					
3.					
4.					
5.					
6.					
7.					
8.					
9.					
10.					
11.					
12.					

Part 3: Equity Strategies

The Equity Framework aims to create balance in improvement efforts. Now that you have listed all of your school improvement programs, initiatives, curriculum, and professional development efforts in Part 2, categorize each of these efforts on the worksheet that follows as culture, practice, or leadership according to the following criteria:

- *Culture*—Does the school improvement effort build an effective learning culture where students and teachers alike are safe in their learning, collaborate, and develop cultural competency wherein they learn about the culture of themselves and their students?
- *Practice*—Does the school improvement effort develop the pedagogical skills of teachers and help them implement effective learning strategies, curriculum alignment and approaches, assessment methods, classroom management, intervention, and general teaching skills?
- *Leadership*—Does the school improvement effort develop vision, direction, and accountability as well as improve the effectiveness, skills, and instructional leadership of administrators, support staff, teacher leaders, and informal leaders?

When listing each school improvement effort, include the plus sign (+), check mark (✓), or minus sign (–) from the "who equitably benefits?" column in the Part 2 table, which shows whether or not the effort creates equity for all students.

Also, based upon your work in Part 1 of this equity lens, include the percentage of time and resources of your school improvement efforts that are dedicated to the three areas of equity support, culture, practice, and leadership.

EQUITY LENS PART 3 WORKSHEET

CULTURE

% of resources:_____
% of time:_____

PRACTICE

% of resources:_____
% of time:_____
Sample:
+ differentiation PD

EQUITY

LEADERSHIP

% of resources:_____   % of time:_____

EQUITY ACTION #6

Based upon your work so far analyzing your own school improvement efforts with an equity lens according to the Equity Framework, determine:

- Are you balanced according to the Equity Framework in the areas of culture, practice, and leadership?
- According to your equity lens, where are your greatest equity strengths based on programs that you labeled with a plus symbol?
- According to your equity lens, where are your greatest equity weaknesses based on programs that you labeled with a minus symbol?

Create a report based on these three questions with recommendations about how to improve equity in your school or school system according to the Equity Framework. Share this report with a supervisor and/or colleagues.

CHAPTER 7

Moral Equity

The challenge with equity is that it is tiring. How can we sustain our efforts when, daily, we are buffeted by resistance, doubt, and a thousand other diversions? The first step in realizing the moral purpose of equitizing schools is not deflecting the work of equity simply because it cuts too deeply and too personally into who you are as an individual, an educator, and an institution. The very day I finished writing this book, I was sitting on a plane next to a White woman. During takeoff, I had been reading the seminal book, *Dismantling Racism,* by Joseph Brandt. The purpose of this book is for White people to challenge the very source of racism—prejudice and power within the White community. The woman saw the title and mentioned to me, "Wouldn't that be nice . . . but it probably will never happen." In response, I began explaining that the book presented a solution—White people figuring out their role in racial inequity. She suddenly cut me off and asked, "Do you like that computer?" referencing the laptop I had just turned on. And with that, our nascent courageous conversation on race was over. She deflected the conversation to something far less personal, something that required no personal responsibility.

A child who is struggling in school does not get to deflect his or her struggle. The child may disengage from school, but the challenge of an inadequate education will stay with this child throughout his or her lifetime. Whether this student is Black, Brown, White, rich, poor, English speaking, or English learning, it is our personal, institutional, and professional responsibility to help this student reconnect with learning, reconnect with school, and pursue his or her dreams empowered to actually reach them. This is the moral purpose of equity—the responsibility to succeed with all students who enter our schools, no matter who they are, what they look like, or where they are from.

What does it mean to a child whose future looks bright? Does it mean that the world is his or hers to succeed in? What power is placed within this child's hands when barriers to success are removed? There is so much in a student's life that a school cannot control, such as family, emotional, and financial stability. But what educators can impact are the six to seven hours each day that the child enters the school and relies upon its educators to prepare him or her for all that life has to offer.

The more marginalized the child, the more the influence that you, the educator, might have upon this child's life. When the learning is sufficient, then the child can make his or her own decision as to what to do in life since education is no longer one of the barriers that must be overcome. In an equitable school, the educators—the adults within the building—have embraced this understanding and maximize their day-to-day time with each child. In an equitable school, failure is inexcusable, and the results are exceptional.

EQUITY PLUS EXCELLENCE

As emphasized throughout the book, equitable schools focus on leading all students to equally high levels of learning. The goal of equity can be described as the *equality of excellence*. According to Charles Willie (2006) in his article "The Real Crisis in Education: Failing to Link Excellence and Equity," "Education should focus neither on cultivating excellence at the expense of equity nor on cultivating equity at the expense of excellence. In a well-ordered society, the goal of education is to seek both excellence and equity because they are complementary. Neither is complete without the other" (p. 16). In an equitable school, students learn what they need thus preparing them to achieve excellence in school, career, and life.

In addressing the moral purpose of equity, the question must be posed:

What is the professional responsibility of an educator to be the catalyst for success for each and every student, especially students who do not fit the dominant norm?

At what point can the nonsuccess of a child in school become acceptable? What student demographic or background justifies a school in saying that they have done enough for a student, and can do no more? How far are the educators within a school expected to go to guarantee all students learn? As it turns out, very far.

EQUITY SUCCESS:
BEHRMAN CHARTER ELEMENTARY

One of the most disruptive events to ever hit a school system in U.S. history was when Hurricane Katrina hit New Orleans in 2005. The hurricane and flooding nearly destroyed one of the most historical and unique cities in North America. It completely shut down the school system—a system that was already considered by some to be the worst in the United States as it perennially failed the large majority of its students—especially students of Color and from poor backgrounds. In the face of such overwhelming crisis, what could be expected of the schools that reopened several months after Katrina hit? What degree of justification would these educators be granted for not succeeding with all their students living in post-Katrina New Orleans? What would the teachers and administrators expect not only of their students, but also of themselves while working in this recovery-minded city?

For one group of educators, they would accept only the very best. According to René Lewis-Carter, principal of Martin Behrman Elementary Charter School,

> As we started here post-Katrina, we did not know what education was going to look like, but we discovered that our children—the children whose stories had not been told—they wanted to be right back here, right back in New Orleans where it was familiar, where it was comfortable in these antiquated buildings that are in desperate need of repair, getting what they need. And that is a solid education and love.

A former elementary principal in New Orleans, René found herself post-Katrina unemployed and far from home. She knew she wanted to return to New Orleans, so she decided to open a school where all kids could succeed. Contacting two other master teachers, Faydra Alexander and Brian Young, they applied to start a charter school in the nascent Algiers Charter School System.

Once approved, these three passionate educators faced insurmountable odds in opening their school. Negotiating between the overlapping and competing school systems—Algiers Charter, the historical New Orleans Unified School District, and the New Orleans Recovery District—they had to fight for everything: a building, students, teachers and staff, resources, desks, and textbooks, as well as contend with different benefactors, detractors, and champions of each school system.

Once they secured the school's location—the historic Martin Behrman Elementary in the Algiers neighborhood of New Orleans, just across the river from the French Quarter—they had only a matter of weeks to find a staff and prepare the building. All they could count on was that the school would open December 15, 2005.

To hire the staff, they were notified of a citywide hiring day. Entering an auditorium with over one thousand teacher applicants, they were told they only had that morning to hire the entire staff—and they were competing with all the other schools just about to open. When given permission, they raced through the aisles pointing at teachers they knew and letting them know they were hired at Behrman. Even these hirings were not secure as most of the teachers had traveled in from out of town and had not yet found new housing in New Orleans.

Next they faced the daunting prospect of preparing the school by December 15. They entered the school only three days before the students' arrival. Upon entry, they discovered that the school had been tightly sealed for several months since Katrina hit. Following protocol, the previous administration had tightly closed every window and door to prepare for the hurricane. But when the flooding hit, it filled the ground floor of the school with several feet of water. Due to the water damage, the ground floor was unusable. But, the upper floors were also damaged because the sealed-in moisture encouraged the growth of mold and mildew on every book and desk, and filled the air with a putrid smell. With no time to spare, this newly formed staff went from classroom to classroom tossing textbooks, desks, and all other debris out the windows onto the ground below. With almost no textbooks and few desks, the staff was ready, just in time, to open.

Before the students arrived, the staff had committed to being prepared for the students not only physically, but emotionally as well. According to Brian, "We took on the hard part of Katrina, and we let the children be children." The school's other master teacher, Faydra, adds that "It had to feel like school, because their world did not feel normal to them at the time."

"Normal" was indeed a strange phenomenon. On opening day, over 75 percent of the incoming students were technically homeless, as were over 50 percent of the teachers. Due to Hurricane Katrina, the staff and students began Behrman Charter with deeply seated trauma and emotionally wrenching experiences.

Herschel Stevenson, a first-grade teacher at Behrman, recalls:

My family and I were separated. My husband's family was separated from us. And my family was separated from me. It was a lot of crying. It was a lot of "we can't find people," and the phones did not work properly. We didn't know what happened. It was just really bad. And then looking at the TV everyday, we must have cried for at least six weeks because you kept seeing children. That was the strangest thing. I had my roll book with me with all of the children's names and phone numbers, and I kept calling and calling and trying to get through. I found not one child, not one parent. And all I could think is, "the kids are gone."

At Behrman Charter Elementary, the goal was to find these children, provide stability, make up for the time these children were out of school, and help them find hope and predictability in their disrupted lives. "After Katrina, all of us were displaced. Many of our teachers came back with no homes to come back to," says Brian. "But we wanted to help rebuild our city, and part of our rebuilding our city was to help our students, because we realized that New Orleans had a future, and that our children are the future."

"I remember the first day we opened," recalls René, "I had no idea what education would look like here at Behrman post-Katrina. But what I did want, I wanted children to leave here, go home, and be able to tell their parents, 'I want to go back to Behrman, tomorrow.'"

And come back they did. The student population of Behrman Charter Elementary is 98 percent African American and 97 percent of students are on free and reduced-price lunch. Many would consider it a success simply to keep these kids in school and show minimal progress over time. But that was insufficient for Behrman's staff. The crisis of Katrina provided these educators with the opportunity to build a school from the ground up and to institutionalize equity at every level. From the beginning, they focused their efforts on high standards, collaboration, and individually supporting the emotional and learning needs of every student.

J'Vann Martin, an administrative intern at the school, explains:

> We have job-embedded professional development that is done during the day where you sit down, not just with your grade level, but you sit down laterally with other grade levels, and you plan together, and you disaggregate data together, and you devise plans on ways to improve student achievement.

Behrman relied on their own skills, talents, and creativity to determine the structure and practices of the school, rather than relying on outside help and consultants. This trust and dependency of their own efforts empowered the educators to personally own the school's improvement efforts.

Emphasizing the simplicity of a complex solution—the *simplicity* of their approach (Kluger, 2008)—René explains, "You just need the good mix of a belief system, climate, and culture. A climate and culture of believing in people, respect and dignity, believing in the children. I believe in their ability to learn. I believe in our teachers' ability to teach." Trusting in the ability of the educators to succeed with each student, René shares the ownership of Behrman Charter's success with all the staff—it is a collective effort year after year.

The success they achieved through this approach is amazing: only two and a half years after opening with all the inherent challenges of recovering from Hurricane Katrina, 98 percent of the fourth-grade students passed at grade level or above on the Louisiana Educational Assessment Program (LEAP) exam—98 percent! Practically the entire fourth grade passed, which is the grade that Louisiana measures in elementary assessments. Not only did the Behrman educators bring stability and love to the lives of these students, they taught them rigorously, held them to high expectations, and led them to one of the highest proficiency levels in Louisiana.

A remarkable example, Behrman profoundly illustrates the principles of equity applied within a school. Cherie Goins, assistant principal, attributes their success to the dedication of the staff in serving every student: "The teachers that we have, working with our kids—[there is] something special about those teachers: a tremendous commitment to making sure that every child does learn. Not on the same day, not in the same way, but making sure that every child achieves."

But at Behrman Charter, educators extend beyond just academic success in their love and caring for students. Faydra illustrates in her own story how personal the work and success at Behrman has become:

> I have a young family [relation] who was relocated post-Katrina in another state. As a young child, she actually survived Katrina in an apartment and then got out at the last minute. She was not ready for school, was not ready to handle the rigors of academics from day to day. But, she was in a school [in another state] where they were doing the best they could, but they just weren't meeting her needs. She didn't feel a part of that school. She didn't feel love; she felt different. She felt she was the one who was "the odd-man out." After talking to her mom, I said, "send her back, send her here [to New Orleans], and I will keep her until school is out." [She came to a] first-grade teacher here who took her traumatized, even afraid when it rained. Afraid of loud noises because she survived what she did. But now, she has blossomed. She loves school. She loves her teacher. She loves books. She loves learning and it's because of what she got here. That has made the difference in her life. That has healed a part of her that no place else could do.

In this act of love and dedication to an individual student, Faydra takes the work of improving school to a much deeper and personal level. In moving far beyond traditional professional responsibility, she dedicated herself not only to the education but also to the very life of a child who was not directly her own. "When it touches your own family, when you say, 'This is the school where my children need to be! Send her to me!'" Faydra continues, "And I say that with a twenty-one-year-old and a fifteen-year-old, and starting all over again with a six-year-old, I was willing to do that because I knew this was the place she needed to be!"

The educators of Behrman Charter Elementary have built a school worthy of their own children. They have personalized their own work as educators for all children—treating each and every student at Behrman as worthy of the same educational opportunities their own children should receive. At Behrman, educational success is the *right* of every child, regardless of who they are or where they come from. As René explains, "I will just not have it said that because the students I serve are poor, or because this building is antiquated and in desperate need of repairs, that we are not achieving."

Working with conviction and great satisfaction, the educators at Behrman created one of the most profound examples of educational success I have personally witnessed. They took a school nearly in ruins, staffed it with displaced educators, served a traumatized and homeless student body and expected the most of them, focused on their practice, dedicated themselves to each individual student, and lifted them to remarkably high levels of achievement.

As illustrated in the equity lens that follows, Behrman Charter Elementary has created an educational institution that fully supports all students in the drive toward equity. Collectively as educational leaders, they implemented with fidelity the best practices in a supportive learning culture so as to fully support each individual student. The results speak for themselves.

Faydra concludes:

At this point, we don't want the nation to look at us as victims. We want them to see us rising, and we are showing victory now. You can see our school, you can see our students, you can see our test scores, and you see what we are doing with Algiers Charter School System. That is victory, and that is what we feel good about, and we are proud to be at Behrman Charter. I don't think you could make us leave.

Figure 7.1   Equity Lens: Behrman Charter Elementary School

CULTURE

Personal Strategies
- Connect personally with every student.
- Commit to the mission and vision of the school.

Institutional Strategies
- Create strong sense of community within the school.
- Build supportive and safe learning environment to support students no matter their challenges out of school.

Professional Strategies
- Schedule and support teacher collaboration.
- Empower teachers to understand and support individual student needs.

PRACTICE

Personal Strategies
- Expect and support excellence in all teaching strategies.
- Reflect data in teachers' instruction and planning.

Institutional Strategies
- Implement best practices in all classrooms with support from master teachers.
- Implement rigorous standards-based instruction.

Professional Strategies
- Provide technique for differentiating the instruction.
- Share effective pedagogical practices in teams and across grade levels.

EQUITY

LEADERSHIP

Personal Strategies
- Emphasize that all educators focus on being the best at their practice.
- Emotionally engage in the total support required by students.

Institutional Strategies
- Institutionalize full support for students no matter what the student's physical, emotional, or academic needs may be.
- Hold high expectations for every student.

Professional Strategies
- Improve practice through master teachers' work with teams and individual teachers.
- Develop ability to analyze and use data to drive teaching improvements.

STARING DOWN FAILURE

Often in education, the schools in greatest crisis become the exemplars of success. Dunbar High in Baltimore faced the threat of reconstitution. Behrman had to recover from Hurricane Katrina. Sanger Unified School District was nearly taken over by the state. In all of these situations, victory came in the face of great trial. Just like the mythological phoenix rises from the ashes, these schools stared down their failure and found triumph in the most desperate of situations.

If these schools facing such great odds eliminated their inequities and lifted all students to high achievement, what are you capable of achieving? What changes need to occur in your practice so that high achievement occurs for all students?

Recently, I worked with a suburban school district that was quite wealthy and well regarded in the state for its success. People deliberately moved to this district so their children could attend its schools. But, like so many similar districts, the school system did phenomenally well with about 85 percent of its students, but could never quite figure out how to succeed with the remaining 15 percent. In analyzing these 15 percent of failing students, the educators determined that they did not naturally fit the dominant norm of this system as measured by race, language, and economics—for whatever reason, these kids did not connect to the school, and the educators struggled to connect with them.

In this situation, how might these educators get past their successes—their institutionalized pride—and figure out their struggles? Just before lunch, we engaged in a conversation about complacency. We talked about the phoenix rising from the ashes in these highly successful schools that had turned around failure, and we discussed how this district need not face such crisis to build equity for all. The key they identified was to personalize the challenge by getting to know each of the struggling students individually.

Will they do it? I have nothing but hope—hope that they will stay engaged, hope that they will not simply rely upon the majority of succeeding students to symbolize success, but rather will count all of their students in their measurement of achievement—especially those who have traditionally not succeeded.

Places such as Behrman Charter Elementary succeed because of the moral purpose—the *moral equity*—that they incorporate into everything they do. Fullan (2003) writes in *The Moral Imperative of School Leadership*:

Let's be explicit. The only goal worth talking about is transforming the current school system so that large-scale, sustainable, continuous reform becomes built in. Moral purpose of the highest order is having a system where all students learn, the gap between high and low performance becomes greatly reduced, and what people learn enables them to be successful citizens and workers in a morally based knowledge society. (p. 29)

If the moral purpose of education is to have a system where all students learn, then is it immoral to fail in this aim? Is it immoral to have certain groups of students succeed when others do not? And what, if any, responsibility does the individual and dedicated educator have in this regard?

All the responsibility. Most students—especially those not currently succeeding—make no choice as to where they attend school. Typically, it is just chance, at best, that gives these students a good teacher here or there. But equity demands more than this—the moral side of equity asks educators to embrace the possibility that all students can be guaranteed an effective education. Terrell and Lindsey (2009) write that "Our schools are crucibles for our diverse society demonstrating that education is a right not a privilege. Together we have a role in making a vision of inclusive education accessible for all demographic groups of students" (p. 112).

Making an effective education a *right* and not a *privilege* requires us collectively as educators to move far beyond our traditional constructs of school. Just because it might have worked for us does not mean it will work for our students. I add my voice to the many voices now saying that an effective education is every student's civil right. The great challenge of equitizing schools is recognizing that an effective school is one that works for each of today's students, not one that matches our own assumptions as to what school should be.

THE JOURNEY BEHIND—THE JOURNEY AHEAD

As I recall my own education, I was the majority—I was the same culturally, racially, ethnically, socioeconomically, and even religiously as 95 percent of my teachers. Both of my parents were teachers, and I was the fourth in a line of successful Linton students.

Success was nearly guaranteed for me. I recently conducted a webinar and asked participants to identify an individual who had personally given them a chance to succeed. A participant responded that never in her life had she *not* experienced anyone doubting her ability to succeed in school. That was my own experience—the assumption of success through twenty years of education.

I was the dominant norm. If I based my understanding of how schools should function today based purely on my own educational experience, I would miss the mark on nearly 50 percent of today's students. With knowledge comes responsibility. Establishing equity as the foundational operational principle of schools guides educators in embracing the growing diversity that is the reality of our schools.

Tim Wise (2010) calls directly upon us to act:

> Standing still is never an option so long as inequities remain embedded in the very fabric of the culture. And both emanate from the realization that we cannot merely wait for the state or political leaders to act. We must take action ourselves. We must act on the recognition of that which we know to be true. We must move ahead and demand justice in our communities and institutions where we operate. (p. 193)

This is the "so what?" the "what now?" and the "where do I start?" of equity work: the need to act now on behalf of *all* students, especially those not succeeding and those from diverse backgrounds. Terrell and Lindsey (2009) finish their book, *Culturally Proficient Leadership,* asking whether or not each of us will:

- Adopt a moral position that all children and youth have the capacity to learn at high levels?
- Make it your business to find ways to educate all children and youth to high levels? (p. 118)

INTERNALIZING EQUITY

Several years ago when I began learning about equity, race, institutionalized racism, and social justice, I believed that my personal sense of professional responsibility toward all students was deeply embedded. I understood that I had inequitably received so much from my own education, and that these same opportunities needed to be institutionalized for all students, especially students who differed from me. And then I became a father of two amazing and beautiful children who did not fit the norm like I did—and my personal commitment to this work dramatically changed.

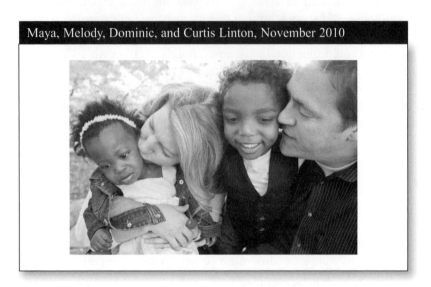

Maya, Melody, Dominic, and Curtis Linton, November 2010

As shared throughout this book, Dominic and Maya are Black, and my wife Melody and I are White. We have found ourselves at the front edge of how race functions currently in society. For one who grew up so much the dominant norm, I have never felt so much outside the norm. I know for a biased fact that these children are fabulous. But society does not quite know how to interpret our young family. Rarely is it disdain that we feel from others. Rather, it is a sense of curious oddity that we experience in the faces of those we pass. We simply are not normed.

What is also not normed is the guarantee of my children's success. This has become internalized for me. It is what drives my moral compass in working for equity for all students. But to accomplish this, their schools cannot function the same way mine did. Their schools need to embrace Dominic and Maya *because* of their difference, not despite it. Until difference is normed, my children will always be a visible symbol of difference.

Currently we live in a school system where Black students score, on average, 40 percentage points below their White counterparts. I work closely with this system and have often asked what would be the best school in the district for my children. More than once, the response has been, "Oh, you don't need to worry. Dominic and Maya have you and Melody as parents—they'll do well." But this is a painfully inadequate response. I don't want to gamble on the fact that my Black children will succeed simply because they have White parents. I want my children to be guaranteed success much like I was. There is no guarantee of their success when it is necessary for my children's teachers to see us, their White parents, in order to believe in Dominic and Maya's learning potential.

I find myself in a disturbing conflict—I am the benefactor of a lifetime of White privilege with all its assumptions of possibility and success, raising Black children in a world that still doubts their potential. The only way I can reconcile this conundrum is for Dominic and Maya to symbolize for me why I am engaged in equity work.

But it is not only Dominic and Maya alone whom I am fighting for—it is for all Black kids who look like them, all Brown kids who bring their own unique racial, language, and cultural differences, and all kids no matter their skin color who don't look like them. It is for every child, no matter their demographic or background. It is for all kids who grow up filled with their own beautifully unique diversity and individuality, for when *any* student can succeed in school no matter their profile, then *all* students can succeed and receive an equitable education. This work is not about me changing the lives of people who are different than me. It is about me changing who I am, and working to change the very institutions and norms that have served me so well so that the privileges I have always received become the norm for everyone.

DRIVING EQUITY

This book began with the story of Northrich Elementary, its principal Sandy Nobles, and the school's success at lifting 100 percent of all students to grade level and above. After Northrich, Sandy became the principal of a very unique school about one mile from downtown Dallas, the J. Eric Johnson Community School (JEJCS). It is a small private lab school where the teachers focus on studying their practice and truly changing the lives of students. They work on specifically identifying what needs to happen to increase student engagement in an urban setting so that all students can succeed. It is a neighborhood school where more than 95 percent of students are Latino, 83 percent qualify for free and reduced-price lunch, and 63 percent speak Spanish at home.

A private foundation funds this school and the school charges only a nominal tuition, as it is focused on serving the surrounding community. Almost every teacher at Johnson Community School began teaching in public schools. Now, they focus on examining their practice, sharing what they learn, working with university researchers, and publishing articles on their practice. According to Sandy, "We are all public school teachers and we are all really interested in learning what can happen in all schools that will make a difference for all kids."

Sandy stresses the need for a similar commitment at Johnson Community School as she did at Northrich:

We are in this together. I take responsibility for things that do not go well, but we all take the glory for the things that go the right way. This is really what has to happen for the trust to be for everybody. Those high expectations need to be clear and concise. If the expectations aren't being met, it has to be addressed. This has to be ongoing. It cannot wait till the next evaluation. . . . If it's not happening, then you have to be very intentional about the consequences, but through the filter that "this is about the work." If you are clear and transparent, you will find more success.

Sandy has led the staff at Johnson Community School on discovering how to lead this primarily Latino school from simply passing to a Texas Commended level, which designates the school as exceeding academic expectations with its student body. The school's goal is to build sustainable educational equity and lifelong success for the students. According to Sandy,

By continually examining practice to meet the developmental needs of each child . . . and by raising expectations for all teachers, students, and families, we have seen results over three and four years such as fifth grade Commended in science moving from 18 percent to 69 percent and fifth grade [Commended in] math increasing from 14 percent to 72 percent in 2010. This data shows that gaps exist for reasons beyond ability. This community school in Dallas believes that children can be highly successful when the educational environment is a student centered, respectful place for families to partner with educators to create better tomorrows for their children.

Equity is about the "tomorrows" for our students and children. Equity provides an educational experience wherein all students can succeed because they are individually accepted, understood, and supported by the educators within the school. With equity, every student owns his or her future. With equity, excellence is found.

EQUITY IN ACTION: CHAPTER 7, MORAL EQUITY

Equity Discussion

With a group, discuss the following: What does moral equity mean to you? What does it look like? In what ways can you define what you currently do as representative of moral equity?

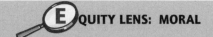

EQUITY LENS: MORAL

Analyze who personalizes equity work for you. Who is the individual—a student, your own child, a family member, even yourself—that symbolizes this quest for equity? Can you identify one or two individuals who represent for you more than simple professional responsibility as an educator? What does the person need in order to experience equity? In describing this personalization of equity, identify what it is you need to do to build equity for all your students.

EQUITY ACTION #7

In your own area of responsibility—be it a classroom, a school, or a district—identify the first three steps you need to take to start establishing equity for all students. Complete these three steps, analyze the process you engaged in, and identify where you need to go next.

Epilogue

The next book of this *Equity 101* series addresses culture.

Equity 101—Book 2: Culture, coauthored with Bonnie Davis, focuses on creating a classroom, school, and system culture where excellence is achieved for every student, and where diversity becomes the norm. Equity can only occur in a culture where it is safe for adults and students alike to take risks, stretch, and learn, and where faculty understand themselves racially and culturally as well as their students. *Equity 101—Book 2: Culture* features:

- Equity culture school success
- Culture within the Equity Framework
- Working definition of equitable culture
- Becoming culturally competent
- Actualizing an equitable learning culture

I look forward to joining you in this journey toward educational equity. Please reach out and keep me informed of your progress and the successful equitable practices you implement. Learn more at www.curiousschool.org, or follow Curious School on Facebook, LinkedIn, and Twitter. You can also contact me at:

Curtis Linton
CEO
Curious School
801-414-7504
curtislinton@curiousschool.org
www.curiousschool.org

References

Blankstein, A. M. (2004). *Failure is not an option: Six principles that guide student achievement in high-performing schools.* Thousand Oaks, CA: Corwin.

Bonilla-Silva, E. (2006). *Racism without racists: Color-blind racism and the persistence of racial inequality in the United States* (2nd ed.). Oxford, UK: Rowman & Littlefield.

Chenoweth, K. (2007). *"It's being done": Academic success in unexpected schools.* Cambridge, MA: Harvard Education Press.

Cortes, C. E. (2002). *The making and remaking of a multiculturalist.* New York: Teachers College Press.

Danielson, C. (2007). *Enhancing professional practice: A framework for teaching* (2nd ed.). Alexandria, VA: Association for Supervision and Curriculum Development.

Darling-Hammond, L. (1997). *The right to learn.* San Francisco: Jossey-Bass.

Davis, B. M. (2006). *How to teach students who don't look like you: Culturally relevant teaching strategies.* Thousand Oaks, CA: Corwin.

Davis, B. M. (2009). *The biracial and multiracial student experience: A journey to racial literacy.* Thousand Oaks, CA: Corwin.

DeCuir, J. T., & Dixson, A. D. (2004, June/July). "So when it comes out, they aren't that surprised that it is there": Using critical race theory as a tool of analysis of race and racism in education. *Educational Researcher,* pp. 26–31.

EDEquity. (2006). *Edwin Lou Javius executive biography.* Retrieved from http://www.edequity.com/about_me.asp

Equity. (2010). In *Merriam-Webster online dictionary.* Retrieved from http://www.merriam-webster.com/dictionary/equity

Fullan, M. (2003). *The moral imperative of school leadership.* Thousand Oaks, CA: Corwin.

Fullan, M. (2010). *Motion leadership: The skinny on becoming change savvy.* Online Course at www.pd360.com. Thousand Oaks, CA: Corwin & School Improvement Network.

Gibbs, J. (2006). *Reaching all by creating Tribes learning communities.* Windsor, CA: CenterSource Systems.

Gruwell, E. (1999). *The freedom writers' diary: How a teacher and 150 teens used writing to change themselves and the world around them.* New York: Doubleday.

Henze, R., Katz, A., Norte, E., Sather, S. E., & Walker, E. (2002). *Leading for diversity: How school leaders promote positive interethnic relations.* Thousand Oaks, CA: Corwin.

Howard, G. R. (1999). *We can't teach what we don't know: White teachers, multiracial schools.* New York: Teachers College Press.

Johnson, R. (2002). *Using data to close the achievement gap: How to measure equity in our schools.* Thousand Oaks, CA: Corwin.

Kluger, J. (2008). *Simplexity: Why simple things become complex (and how complex things can be made simple).* New York: Hyperion Books.

Lindsey, R. B., Nuri Robins, K., & Terrell, R. D. (2003). *Cultural proficiency: A manual for school leaders* (2nd ed.). Thousand Oaks, CA: Corwin.

Littky, D., & Grabelle, S. (2004). *The big picture: Education is everyone's business.* Alexandria, VA: Association for Supervision and Curriculum Development.

McIntosh, P. (1989, July/August). White privilege: Unpacking the invisible knapsack. *Peace and Freedom,* pp. 10–12.

Reeves, D. B. (1996–1997). *Making standards work: How to implement standards-based assessments in the classroom, school, and district* (2nd ed.). Denver, CO: Center for Performance Assessment.

School Improvement Network. (2007–2010). *Who Says? Motivational Video Series.* Midvale, UT: School Improvement Network.

Singleton, G., & Linton, C. (2006). *Courageous conversations about race: A field guide for achieving equity in schools.* Thousand Oaks, CA: Corwin.

Terrell, R. D., & Lindsey, R. B. (2009). *Culturally proficient leadership: The personal journey begins within.* Thousand Oaks, CA: Corwin.

Video Journal of Education (VJE). (2006). *No excuses! How to increase minority student achievement.* Midvale, UT: School Improvement Network.

Willie, C. V. (2006). The real crisis in education: Failing to link excellence and equity. *Voices in Urban Education: Equity After Katrina, 11*(10).

Wise, T. (2010). *Colorblind: The rise of post-racial politics and the retreat from racial equity.* San Francisco: City Lights Books/Open Media Series.

Index

A SAGE Publishing Company

Helping educators make the greatest impact

CORWIN HAS ONE MISSION: to enhance education through intentional professional learning.

We build long-term relationships with our authors, educators, clients, and associations who partner with us to develop and continuously improve the best evidence-based practices that establish and support lifelong learning.